Advance Prai

"Read *All My Relations* an~~~~ ways that will bring you to tears, laughter, and what life is truly about."

— Dr. Bernie Siegel, author of *365 Prescriptions for the Soul*

"Through the example of her own life, Susan Chernak McElroy reveals the depth that is possible in our connections with animals and invites us to join her on the journey to reunite with all creation and heal our planet."

— Marta Williams, author of *Learning Their Language*

"Susan Chernak McElroy guides readers through ten eloquent stories and practices that open the heart of the reader to an ancient way of being, *Mitakuye Oyasin,* a Lakota phrase describing kinship with all life. She demonstrates so clearly through her delicious wordsmithing the transformative potential of fostering sacred relations with four-leggeds, winged ones, and indeed, all of Creation. Susan lives this path, breathes it, dreams it, and invokes it to awaken inside each of us."

— Frank MacEowen, Celtic shamanic guide and author of *The Mist-Filled Path* and *The Spiral of Memory and Belonging*

"Two resonances emerge for me in reading *All My Relations.* One is Susan McElroy's storytelling, the way of the teacher. Her curricula are breathtaking. The second is the stuff of life, so incisively and poetically expressed as to evoke for me the Creation, dressed in its stunning mathematics."

— Leon M. Lederman, winner of the Nobel Prize in Physics and author of *The God Particle*

All My
Relations

All My Relations

Living with
Animals
as Teachers
and Healers

SUSAN CHERNAK McELROY

Illustrations by Connie Bowen

NEW WORLD LIBRARY
NOVATO, CALIFORNIA

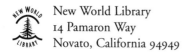 New World Library
14 Pamaron Way
Novato, California 94949

Illustrations by Connie Bowen
Text design and typography by Tona Pearce Myers

Library of Congress Cataloging-in-Publication Data
McElroy, Susan Chernak
  All my relations : living with animals as teachers and healers / Susan Chernak McElroy.—1st ed.
     p.   cm.
  ISBN 1-57731-430-1 (pbk. : alk. paper)
  1. Human-animal relationships. 2. Animals—Psychological aspects.
3. Pets—Psychological aspects. 4. Pet owners—Psychology. I. Title.
  QL85.M329 2004
  158.1—dc22   2004012471

First printing October 2004
ISBN 1-57731-430-1

 Printed in Canada on 100% postconsumer waste recycled paper

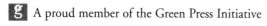 A proud member of the Green Press Initiative

Distributed to the trade by Publishers Group West

10   9   8   7   6   5   4   3   2   1

To those who have always embraced all of Creation as family
and have often felt like resident aliens because of it:
Welcome home.

Contents

Gratitudes

Nothing of consequence in our lives happens outside the bowl of relationships. Certainly this is true of the making of books. So the writing of this page is the most fun part of the publishing process for me — the part where I come up close and sweet beside my gratitude and thanksgiving:

Thank you, New World Library, for allowing me to get another book out there in the world. Thank you, Georgia Hughes, my wonderful editor, for working with me in such a mysterious, collaborative, brainstorming sort of way — a way that leaves me open to the writing process and confident all through it. Thank you Connie Bowen, my friend and illustrator, for bringing my most precious relations back to life through your pen. Many thanks to my fine bulldog of an agent, Elaine Markson, who continues to find homes for my book ideas.

My gratitudes to my support network of friends and family are especially heartfelt. All supported me through a mind-dismembering clinical depression that stalked me for two years and could have easily eaten me whole. And so, thank you, RiverWind Foundation, for inviting me to share my work through the context of a committed organization of like-hearted teachers, healers, and passionate dreamers.

Thank you to my Spirit Family — blood is thicker than water, but love is thicker than blood. Thank you for the loving gift of community that I am only beginning to understand in its deeper, more sacred context. Many, many heartfelt gratitudes to my beloved friend Tim O'Donoghue. You hold me to my highest call, and I bless you for seeing me with larger eyes than I can see myself. Thank you also to my Sundance Family and my Kindred Spirit Community. As I write these words, I am astonished and humbled at the enormity of the support that enfolds me from all corners of the world.

A most grateful thank you to Fritz Saam, friend and gentle first reader. Whenever I question myself and my work, you remain my champion, my advocate.

Thank you to my current animal family — Strongheart, Arrow, Mirella — and to all my relations who have walked beside me all along the way, bringing me lessons sometimes at great risk to themselves.

A special thank you to my mother, Hermine. At eighty-one, you are my nearest and dearest Wisdom Keeper, an elder and a *heyoka* all rolled into one.

Thank you, thank you, each and all, for the dance.

Introduction

This is a book of ten personal stories, ten reflections, and ten practices that combine to form a prayer. Not the kind of prayer we say with our eyes closed and our heads bowed, but one that asks us to *be* the prayer, every moment of every day. This is prayer not in a formal, religious sense, but in a lived sense. Gandhi said once, "To have peace, then be peace." This is that kind of prayer.

This prayer asks nothing less than our complete devotion and attention, and for the enormous commitment it seeks from us, it offers back nothing less than the full healing of our selves and of all the world. Think of this book, then, as an offering of wishes, supplications, and thanksgiving in story form that acts as a sacred container for the keeping and living of this prayer. The prayer itself is only three words, yet encoded within these few words lies the mending of our relationship with all of life. The prayer is simple and huge, and I offer it to you with love and urgency.

The Prayer

The drums ceased and the firekeeper flung open the door to the sweat lodge. I'd been sitting cross-legged and bent over for nearly three hours with fifteen other people in the dark, hot, womb-like blanketed dome, praying according to Lakota tradition. I had just finished my first sweat lodge. "Say 'Mitaku Oyasin' and kiss the ground before you leave the lodge," David Bearclaw, the lodge chief, whispered to me. I bent down, pressed my lips to the wet dirt, said something like "meetak-weeyasa," and groped my way out to the daylight. David called after me, "'Meeta'koo-weya'sin.' It is a Lakota phrase meaning 'all my relations,' or 'all my relatives.' It's a way of honoring everything." He paused for a moment and then added, "It's a prayer."

The phrase followed me out of the lodge that day, haunting and succinct. It follows me still. "All My Relations." If humankind lived as though all of creation were honored relations, the world would be healed overnight. Concise and beautiful, *Mitaku Oyasin* encapsulates my personal prayer for animals and the Earth: That they be to us as relatives.

I've been told that *Mitaku Oyasin* has an even larger meaning than "All My Relations." Although this seems to be the closest translation English can offer, Tony Ten Fingers, an Oglala man, offers a deeper definition of the phrase. As

my author and brother-friend Frank MacEowen passed on
to me, "Tony says if you look at the word 'Mitaku' or
'Mitakuye,' it literally means 'everything': the birds, the deer,
the dew, the rain, the thunder, the spirits, the peoples of all
nations, the past, the future, the galaxies, death, life, harmony, war, light, darkness — 'Mitakuye' is so vast that it
contains it all.

"'Oyasin' means 'to invoke an unyielding, unwavering,
contagious spirit that inspires everyone to learn all we can.'
Tony says that in the Lakota tongue, 'Oyasin' means 'the
contagious spirit of learning,' but not just head-learning. It
also means heart-learning, soul-learning, and spirit-learning.
'Mitaku Oyasin' really means to invoke a contagious spirit
that inspires us to learn all we can know about everything. In
this way, it becomes a prayer unto itself that never excludes."

I am intimately familiar with exclusion. In part, I know
that my own relationship with animals and nature, wind and
fire, was my child-inspired antidote to certain kinds of alien-
ation. I was born in a high-rise New York City apartment
and moved three years later to a series of trailers and apart-
ments and then to a tiny house in a factory town suburb. You
might think my contact with animals and nature would be
very limited there, but I found both because I needed both.
We had a parakeet, a fish tank, salamanders under the stones
in the yard, birds at the feeder, and the occasional visiting
opossum. There was a regional park where I could see garter
snakes, polliwogs, some deer and raccoons, plus a small
trickle of a creek.

I was an awkward child with an odd assortment of challenges that drew attention to me in ways no child would ever

choose. I lisped badly. I stuttered as I lisped. My eyes wandered in different directions, much like the googly eyes of a stuffed toy, and I wore a pair of glasses with lenses thick as saucers. Top that off with the fact that I was skinny as a flamingo leg, and you have a picture of a child who got a fair amount of comment on the playground, little of it good. My comfort with animals and nature was a healing balm to me. No polliwog ever laughed at me. No parakeet ever waited, fidgeting, as I struggled to finish a sentence. Even though my throat refused to voice what I had to say, the wind understood me and cradled me, wordlessly.

I remember one evening overhearing my mother in the kitchen below innocently tell her friend, in reference to my enchantment with animals, "Susie will be outgrowing these things soon enough." I was always taking in some helpless animal; that evening a nest of orphaned blackbirds sat in a shoe box atop our stove. It could just as easily have been a sick kitten, or a hurt toad. "Instead of birds and kittens," Mom sighed, "it'll be boyfriends and cars."

But I never did "outgrow it," and so I assumed, shamefacedly, that I never "matured." The cultural voice that dismisses the deep connection most children share with animals and nature is often a voice without any words at all, but these can be the most influential voices of all: a look, a giggle, a turned back, a patronizing wink. I know from my own experience — and from the words of hundreds of readers who tell me they felt like aliens all their lives — that life can be isolating and painful for the many who have always carried this truth: We are related to all of life.

The Memory

Even though it is ignored and undervalued in our society, the world view that honors and invokes wisdom from animals and nature has been held by more than an unusual few. In fact, probably no longer than five thousand years ago, All My Relations was the universal philosophy espoused by humankind. In a time when we knew how to participate less catastrophically in the family of life, leaving no insanity, garbage, or holocausts in our wake, All My Relations was the lived prayer that kept us safe on Earth, and Earth safe in us. If we invoke it now, earnestly, it may keep us safe again.

We sprang from the living world. Every five to seven years, the molecules in our bodies go back to nature, and nature in turn supplies us with hers. We are each literally and spiritually reborn again and again in our lifetime, from our atoms on up. We are related to Earth through our bodies, our minds, and our spirit. We remember her in our bones and muscles and mind. Yet over the centuries, we have distanced ourselves from animals and nature, and our tools for living have diminished in direct proportion to the degree of our separation from the wisdom and healing of the living Earth. Ecopsychologist Michael Cohen writes, "We need tangible contact with real nature to recover from our traumatic, mental detachment from it. With Nature, as with God, only the real thing is good enough. Only Nature has the power to regenerate what our detached thinking has torn asunder....The natural world, materially and feelingly, is your subconscious mind."[1]

I agree completely. Remembering our ancestral world

view, whose center pole is reverence and awe, is critical to human life and well-being. I am absolutely clear in my conviction about this. On a flight out of Idaho Falls this past summer, my seat mate, a university professor of geology, began speaking to me about the state of world affairs. My position was that most squirrels and ducks live better lives than most people. In his engaging and animated response, he argued that the technological marvels of medicine, machines, and life extension prove that we live far better than squirrels and ducks. I asked him, "How many people do you know, personally, who are at peace with their lives and with the way the world is?" The professor looked up at the ceiling of the plane, paused, and said, "Boy, not many."

Medicine, airplanes, computers, and democracy are fine things. I rely on them all, but I do not rely on them for meaning. I know better. In August of 1988, I was in a hospital having surgery for a cancer I was told would be terminal. Waking up from the operation two hours later in a rank fog of anesthesia, I experienced a series of visceral moments, knotted to each other like a string of pearls, during which I came to know exactly and completely what is important to life. It is just one thing: relationships. All kinds of relationships. Relationships with everything and everyone. Meaning is not to be found in medicine or technology or even life extension, but in the blessing and the agony of relationships. I understood beyond question that the full value of my life culminates in those gracious and challenging moments of connection. No growth or joy has ever come to me outside of the cradle of relationship, and it never will.

The natural world that has always been so precious to me

is all about healthy, balanced relationships. Our close connections with our animal companions reflect much of that harmony. Most of us know in our hearts that the healthiest and happiest half of a human-dog relationship is the dog. Dogs are still connected to nature, and they bring the balance of that connection into their lives with us. Beyond the circle of the domestic animals we love and know, all of wild nature offers us a reflective model for harmony and cooperation and communion. To tune back into that relational system is the greatest gift of pure potential and soul mending we can ever give ourselves. When we forget — and millions of us have forgotten — that the landscape of relationship includes infinitely more possibilities than only human-to-human relationships, we reduce our potential for healing and inner growth tenfold. It is time to remember that relationship is a bigger arena. Perhaps when we do remember this, we can begin to live life as well as a dog, a duck, or a squirrel.

The Journey

Because All My Relations is a prayer not espoused in our Western culture and therefore not taught, we need to begin this relearning on our own. Thankfully, there are many tools that can lead us back to a richer and more deeply felt sense of this close, healing relationship we share with all the living world. This book is one of them: a guided, many-leveled sacred journey designed to deepen our prayer for All My Relations. I wrote it to stimulate both thought and feeling because I know from experience that transformation of consciousness takes both. Sometimes it is a thought that brings us to a feeling we never knew lived in us, and we are changed inside and out. Sometimes it is the feeling that grabs us first, transforming us as we make meaning of the feeling with our thoughts and reflections.

Although I was born loving animals and the outdoors, my relationships with them have deepened profoundly only as I have put my attention and intention behind those relationships. As studies on the healing power of prayer point out, it is not the words of the prayer but the intention and the earnestness put into it that ignite the spirit of healing in some mysterious way. No matter how strong our love of animals and nature, we all can and must deepen our prayer.

Exploring relationships with animals, Earth, and each other is a pilgrimage with no final destination. In my writing I have revisited over and over again many concepts and conflicts about these relationships that continue to confound me. Since I wrote *Animals as Teachers and Healers* in 1996, I have grown old enough to know that we never know anything once and for all. "Once and for all" is a grandiose notion we should release in our lives, as one would release a seedpod to the wind. We are not charged by life to complete our soul's journey, only to honor and to deepen it.

Shamans say that it is not wise or safe to take someone on a journey to a place you have never been. This book reflects honestly where I have been on my journey. The tools I share with you are those that have helped me most in my own life: story, reflection, and practice. Story taps into the emotion and soul of transformation. Reflection feeds the mind and spirit. Practice — putting our hands and bodies to something

— is the embodiment, the doing, of life. I used to argue with myself about which of these was the most important, which was the arena where I should be spending most of my life's energies. Should I be, think, or do? Which was the highest human endeavor? The answer is not one or another, but yes, yes, and yes.

Story

Stories are a gift unique to humankind; we have been story-tellers since the dawning of our time. Storytelling is hard-wired in us, something we are irresistibly impelled to do. Story is a powerful tool for feeling our way through concepts and ideas that are too big, too important, and sometimes too bafflingly paradoxical to be grasped in more rational or linear ways. It is no mystery that much of what survives of humankind across time is myth, legend, and story.

Though I love myths and folktales and am awed by the transcultural and transpersonal magnetism of this form of storytelling, I am most personally drawn to personal, con-temporary story. Stories from today, from this time, bring me a special feeling of connection and hope for my own life lived right now. There is something about a personal story that unites me to the storyteller, and to myself, in a nearly mystical way. The quality I treasure most in personal story, I believe, is its intimacy. The enfolding sense of communion I find in personal story is a rich, nourishing gift in a painfully isolated world. And of equal importance to this intimacy is the fact that even as I have lived my own story, so has the teller lived his story, or hers.

The ten stories in this book are my stories, a selection from the stories that have molded my personal history and deepened my inquiry into the prayer of All My Relations. They are the stories that asked to be included, the ones whose memories most call to me in these times, and I trust that they are the ones that most need to be told right now.

Trust in the power of story can enhance its ability to move, inspire, and transform, but story works whether you believe in it or not. Story has an uncanny, unfailing, and evolutionary ability to settle quietly and utterly below the level of the analytical mind. Down below the "How come?" "What if?" and "But why?" a story rests and sings, delighting the Mind behind the mind. This is the precious realm of Mind within us that can actually touch and know the truly important things in life, its confounding intangibles that always float beyond — or beneath — the levels of fact and research, intangibles like love, compassion, belonging, self, devotion, true courage, true calling.

After each story I share in this book, I offer a reflection, often painted with other stories that pertain to it in an important way. These reflections do not claim to impart the essence of the story, just one possible meaning. All of the stories are complete within themselves. Each contains many levels of complexity, and each invites you to journey as deeply or as simply as you choose. You may also decide not to read the reflections that follow each story until you have absorbed the story in your own way and in your own time. We all may find our own meaning in a story. Or we may not. Some stories will strike our souls; some won't.

Reflection

The themes explored in the pages to come are all worthy of not only a first reflection but also much deeper exploration. Each theme is a topic for inquiry and embodiment that can never be completed in a lifetime, and each is essential to more fully come home to the prayer of All My Relations. Combined, these explorations lay a conceptual grounding for shape-shifting into a life of greater awareness, wisdom, healing, and sustaining community.

Through the reflective process, with each concept ushered in by an animal rebirthed in story, I am inviting you to remember what already dwells within you, the gift of conscious reason that nature bestowed upon each of us at birth. We humans have a unique ability to change our minds in big ways. We call this free will, and it is a slippery thing. So far in our evolution, we have not learned how to manage this huge gift well. Recall, for example, my conversation with the geology professor — How many people do you know who are content with their lives, their choices, and the way things are? How many squirrels do you know who aren't?

The reflective essays in this book beckon you to reconsider and reframe the ideas you may hold that limit your ability to feel contentment and peace in and belonging to the world. When supported by the mysterious emotional reconstruction of story, reflection can help us make the leap to a new way of perceiving, which is the catalyst for a new way of living.

Practice

Story opens our hearts, and reflection opens our minds. Practice puts into flesh the quickening of fresh hearts and open minds. The world and each of us is healed when we embody, or "do," our lives. The process of putting our hands to and on something changes the face of the Earth one touch at a time. Hand to Earth, hand to one another. Foot to first step, foot to journey, foot to rest. To use our bodies in doing is to make creation and consciousness manifest. Practice is the concrete step in living any prayer.

Each chapter in this book ends with an activity for you to try. These are the processes that have transformed my own life. A word of advice: The practices I share in this book look deceptively simple — so simple, in fact, that you may be inclined to "imagine" your way through them, rather than doing them. From experience with these processes over time, however, I can tell you that they are not as simple as they seem — to do them and to imagine doing them are universes apart. It is like the difference between reading the recipe and baking the bread. Please try a few, and you will see for yourself. Many hold the key to powerful growth if you will enter the process with an open mind and heart and just do it.

We all have techniques that work best for our own unique method of learning, and I encourage you to arrange what I have offered in any way that works for you. Make the questions into affirmations, turn the activities into meditations, try living some of the concepts in the stories, find a unique way to tell your own stories. If it assists you in your own journey, I invite you to share your reflections in writing

with me at my Website. I would very much like to know
what practices and ideas resonate with you or help you to see
in a new, fresh way. However you do it, take time with this
book. It is not meant to be absorbed in one sitting.

I call you now on a journey into the heart of All My Relations, this most inclusive, remarkable, dynamic prayer. It is a
soul prayer, a healing prayer whose time has come and gone
and come again. Take these stories, reflections, and practices
— each a small and fervent prayer of its own — and offer
them up. Then listen, closely. On the wind, in your cat's eye,
over the waters of a singing river, you will hear the prayer
whispered back — a love song to you from all of creation.

Susan Chernak McElroy
Teton Valley, Idaho
March 2004

Misty

It was a long time before I knew her name, so at first I just called her "the pussycat." We had been living in a small, San Diego trailer park for several weeks before she made herself known to us. Some of her story is hard to remember, because I was only four years old then. I had just started wearing my hair in "pinktails," my own word for the short braids my mother plaited into my straight brown hair each morning. But much of my memory of Misty is as crystal clear to me as the air in Southern California was in those days.

Trailer park living in the late fifties was then as it remains today: The domiciles were not and could not be called "mobile homes" or "coaches," and the term "park" was used not to describe the looks of the place, but rather what you did

there with your trailer. My father was a cook then, a chef years later, and he and my mother had decided to try and assemble a life on the West Coast. Since all my German aunts and uncles lived in San Diego, it seemed as good a place as any to start, and so my New York City apartment days ended with a three-day train trip out west in the middle of summer.

For the next few years, home was an eight-by-thirty-eight-foot yellow and white trailer that moved along with us from park to park as my father searched for good, steady work. When I look at old black-and-white pictures from those days — the kind that came in those small cardboard folders with saw-tooth edging — I am amazed that we all fit in that trailer for so long. My father was tall and big-footed, my brother is no shrimp, and my mom is slender but not petite. I slept in the hallway in a top bunk above my brother, and my parents were crammed into the real-wood-paneled cubby hole of a bedroom in the back. Between us was a bathroom so small that even I could reach from the toilet to the sink — my first memory of multitasking.

I loved my bunk bed. It felt like an indoor tree house. One night, I dreamed I was a fledgling robin in a nest, and Mother Bird was chirping to me to "jump, jump!" When I opened my eyes, it was early morning with the sun glancing off the narrow hall, and I was perched on the railing of the bunk, ready to take my first flight. Apart from the sleeping dreams, I carried with me one special waking dream that I shared with my family if not every night then at least weekly, and several times a day as holidays approached.

In my special dream, "someone" had left for me a small, black kitten in the closet across from the bunk beds. I thought if I told that dream loudly enough, vividly enough, and often enough, "someone" would hear it, and answer.

As it turned out, someone did eventually hear me, but the someone didn't quite get all the particulars straight. The cat who came to us was no kitten, was not black, and did not show up in the closet. Mom says I was never a fussy child, and so I was of course delighted to take any cat, of any color, from anywhere that someone chose to send her to me. At the time, I thought she must have been sent by Jesus. Now I believe the someone who sent her was the cat herself.

Teepee Trailer Park, where we were living at that time, was separated from a line of more elegant, colorful mobile homes by a tall cyclone fence. All these mobile homes had covered back porches and tiny lawns that faced our trailers. Our park had no shade, except for the striped awnings some trailers sported, and no grass. Running the length of the cyclone fence was a shallow concrete gutter, which I adopted as a makeshift river on hot days, when it would be filled by the lawn sprinklers on the "fancy" side of the fence.

That was where I first met the pussycat. Stooped over my river, I was pushing a paper boat down the little stream when I felt something brush my back. I turned to see the yellow eyes of a slender cat, even with my own. Instinctively, I froze. The only cats I had seen in my life were the feral cats who lived in our New York City dumpsters, and they had taught me that swift moves made for swift flight. But this was no feral cat. She was calm, still, curious, and eager to sniff my hands and elbows. She gently rubbed her delicate head against my knee. Her face glowed with grace and knowing. From her presence alone, from her sensuousness, I knew she was a "she."

The pussycat's whiskers were as long as grass stems, and just as soft. She was the loveliest color — a soft gray tabby with narrow zebra-like stripes. Of course, I told myself this was the kitten who was supposed to be in my closet. She was larger than I anticipated, but that was no stumbling block as far as I was concerned, and the stripes were fine — good, really.

Still in my low crouch, I extended my hand and began backing with painstaking deliberateness toward our trailer. I could scarcely believe it when she followed along at a trot, tail up. My mind was racing ahead to the milk I knew we always had in the refrigerator. Along the way, I was struggling to invent some story to tell my mother about how I just knew the pussycat had come to be ours. I was prepared to say anything to convince my family and myself that this was indeed my dream cat come true.

Yet this was to be one of the few times in my life I can remember when the resistance I imagined, and then perhaps evoked, was not there. Mom met us at the trailer steps in flat shoes and an ankle-length skirt. Crouching low, she called to the cat in her softest baby talk, and the pussycat met her out-stretched hand with a rumbling purr. "Hello, pretty one," my mother cooed. "Who do you belong to?" I blurted out that it would be really good if she could belong to us, since she had been sent by Jesus. Mom smiled and stepped backward into the trailer, and I heard the refrigerator door click open.

I want to be able to find the perfect words to explain how the click of the refrigerator door brought all the heavens down upon me with a wild and raging surge of sheer child power. You've had moments like that, too, haven't you? Moments where dreams collide with reality at a perfect intersect point, and you feel as though somehow you have made magic happen?

We call this "magical thinking" and tell ourselves and our children that wishing does not make it so, and that our thoughts do not make things happen. But haven't you had moments when you knew you had done it? You had thought it and it was made true? Well, this was the first time I knew I had done it. I had called the pussycat to me, and Jesus had made it so by the power of my desire. And then to top it off, the huge, otherworldly strength of my thoughts had propelled Mom trance-like to the refrigerator for a bowl of milk! I had done this. I could do anything. I was in control of the uni-verse. I knew it. I was exhilarated and terrified at the same time, and very full of myself, too.

So imagine my shock when Mom explained to me that

this pussycat looked far too well-fed to be needing a new home. Imagine my disbelief when she said that this pussycat could visit, but could not live with us. I stood there on the porch, watching the cat wipe the last of the milk off her whiskers with a gracefully curved paw, and I felt the heavens collide in my young brain. Confusion, frustration, rage, hopelessness, numbness.

Make no mistake about it — I had felt the power. It was real and true. I had been the creatress for a divine instant. The pussycat was mine. Wasn't she? Even now, the proof remained in the form of my mother at the kitchen sink, washing an empty milk bowl — the bowl I had invoked. But now the cat was turning her back to us, tail arched into a question mark, and sliding like smoke under the trailer. I sat on the porch, spent, all my soul-circuits blown, and saw her turn once and look into my eyes with amusement. Her ears flicked. Then she was gone.

But not for long. The next morning, I awoke to a faint but insistent mewing. At first, I imagined it was coming from the hall closet — hallelujah! — but no, she was waiting at the front door. I held open the screen, and she rushed past me and headed directly toward the back bedroom. She knows this place, I told myself. She knows our house. Picking up speed at the end of the hall, she vaulted onto my parent's bed, landing with a purr I could hear all the way into our living room. I heard my mom laugh and my dad grunt, and I ran in to join them. Atop the covers, the pussycat was humming loudly and doing something I had never seen. Her whiskers were pulled forward in a slight pucker, and she was bent from the shoulders, pushing her paws forward and back on my mother's quilt-covered chest. I leaned close to her small cat face, and saw that her eyes were near closed in bliss, and that a small droplet of drool hung like a crystal from her lip.

"What is she doing?" I whispered to my mom. My father chuckled, "Suwee" — his forever name for me — "she's making patti-paws."

I can still feel that morning, all soft and sleepy with the sounds of cat feet treading the quilt with a comforting swish-swish, and my parents giggling, and the love twinkling around the room like invisible stars. And there were many more mornings just like it, with the pussycat appearing regularly and hurrying in to "make bread" on my parents' bed.

Sometimes she came at midday and visited with me. I would pretend she was my baby and wrap her in scarves and carry her around for hours, and she would lay back like a princess, as heavy and relaxed in my arms as a water balloon. Sometimes, caught up in the wonder of her fluid-like body, I would curl up with her and relax every muscle, and we would nap, intertwined and loose-limbed like two cotton ropes. She taught me what a good stretch really is and how to flex your toes and yawn until your mouth is as big as the rest of your face.

Because the pussycat was my pretend baby and babies do not have whiskers, I took the liberty one day of clipping them all off. I thought it made her look rather elegant and streamlined. My mother was horrified, and told me that now the pussycat would not be able to crawl through tight spaces because her whiskers were her "feelers."

I felt wretched about what I had done. It was not the first time, nor would it be the last time in my childhood that I did something that was hurtful without meaning to. I believed that when I was a grown-up, such things would not happen anymore because I would know better. But I still don't. I am over fifty now, and I tell myself that perhaps when I am dead and on the other side I will know better.

"Her name is Misty," my mom told me one afternoon. "She lives in the house just across from us, over there." Her finger pointed to a blue and white mobile home with bright green carpet tacked neatly on a back porch covered with wavy, fiberglass panels. My heart clenched.

The remains of my child-power shriveled up like a prune, locked to those words that were telling me that the pussycat never was mine, never ours. I had only imagined I had done it, that I had conjured her, beckoned her, called her with the power of lightning flashing from my fingertips. I could hear Jesus laugh.

"Her owner says we can share her... Misty," Mom continued. "She knows Misty comes to visit, and she's happy to share." I hung my head and felt my pinktails brush against my cheek. Tears dribbled off the tip of my nose. Forgive me, Jesus. I was not happy to share. It felt wrong. Misty was not to be shared. But no one but me seemed to feel this sense of imminent doom. Certainly not Misty, who continued her morning visits like clockwork. Certainly not my mom, who set out the milk dish on the back porch each day.

Many days later, I curled up in a small aluminum folding chair out back with Misty of the Two Worlds. Her whiskers were beginning to grow back, and they prickled like a hairbrush against my arm where she rubbed her head. She was not a cat who was afraid to look anyone in the eye. Often she would hold my gaze with her golden eyes, and it would be I who turned away from the intensity of our wordless communion. She carried her soul in her eyes, an old soul saturated with life, peace, and an aura of delightful wisdom. This day, her paws worked in ceaseless, luxurious patti-paws, and her purr rumbled in my chest. In the fleeting spaces between the beauty of those precious moments of simple presence — the silkiness of fur; the slant of the afternoon sun; the smell of hot, dry pavement; the sweet, anchor-shaped smile of black cat lips — my mind created and dismissed tactics for assuming full ownership of this cat. All the ideas had their holes, their fatal flaws. Kidnapping Misty and running away from home seemed about the best alternative, and at only four, I couldn't see any long-term success in it.

"The other person has kept her long enough. They don't love her as much as we do. It's time for her to be ours now. She would rather be ours." These were the kinder thoughts I harbored about my shared-cat conundrum. Childhood passions can be raw ones, red and crazy ones. They come from a space of less domestication, before culture has entirely overtaken us, and they are full of creative juice, tender and dripping as a fresh wound. With a final cavernous yawn and a curl of her tail into that characteristic question mark, Misty slipped off my lap in the late day shadows and skipped away.

So very far away.

The next morning, she did not come to the door. Nor the next. My frantic pleadings sent my mother to the cyclone fence for a whispered conversation with the neighbor. Mom returned with her lips tight. Misty was dead. She had been curled up sleeping in the wheel-well of her other family's car when the woman drove off to work in the early morning, jamming on her brakes when she heard the shriek and the thump as Misty's body rolled completely beneath the tire.

I was inconsolable, bereft, literally sick to my stomach with grief. Except for a tiny frog and one goldfish, this was my first experience with tragic death, any death. I was not able to see the pussycat's body, or to participate in her burial. She had been taken to the dump after being wrapped in a plastic bag and placed in the trash. I had no concrete proof of her parting, except for her absence from our door. Sometimes I told myself that they were hiding her. It was a comforting and enraging thought. I even called for her at the cyclone fence for several days, self-consciously, my voice just above a whisper.

But worse than the pain of the loss — if anything can be worse than the pain of that loss — were my feelings of rage and anger at Misty's family for killing her, and at my own family for not taking me seriously when I tried to tell them that something about sharing Misty was not right. She would not have died in my care. I could have kept her safe. I can keep anything safe. This was my childhood credo, my vow, my truth.

Indeed, as the weeks of missing her slipped by, there hardened in me a deep belief in certain paradoxical truths and lies. In four short years I had formed for myself, as every child does, an interior culture made up from the bits and pieces of my life and its stories and from the silent language and urges of my own soul. Fusing soul and story for me in her own unique way, Misty was the bestowing vehicle for certain powerful conceptions created at the time of her life and loss that

I would take with me for many, many decades — concepts I came to life to explore, embody, and transcend.

These, as plainly as I can say them, are the beliefs that Misty ushered into my life: That I am both all-powerful and, at the same time, powerless as a speck of dust. That anyone, anything, is safe ever after in my care. And that nothing — myself included — resides entirely in my care.

These concepts would loom before me for years, like a blackened lighthouse, calling me to slam upon the rocks and sink or to relight the tower — whichever I was capable of at that moment in life. I have many memories of both, mostly of slamming against the rocks and sinking. But sometimes I have felt as though I were holding up a fragile torch high in the sea winds, finally and torturously touching the candle wick at the top of the lighthouse stairs and sending brilliant light cascading into tens of thousands of handmade glass lenses that lit up the ocean with the color of a cat's yellow eyes.

These beliefs still reside inside of me, sometimes like black boulders of clotted lava, sometimes like flashes of brilliant light. They rest like a cat curled on my lap, and when life sends me crashing to the rocks with questions about power, control, and responsibility, these beliefs press like patti-paws on my chest, comforting, irritating, inviting, challenging. The rocks beneath the lighthouse are black-with-gray, and the waves rise over them in a curl like a question mark. These are the colors and textures painted for me as a child, and when the waves break and settle again, they are gray and Misty.

Remembered Relations

HONORING OUR FIRST STORIES

"Remember only this one thing," said Badger. "The stories people
tell have a way of taking care of them. If stories come to you,
care for them. And learn to give them away when they are needed.
Sometimes a person needs a story more than food to stay alive.
That is why we put these stories in each other's memory.
This is how people care for themselves."

— Barry Lopez, *Crow and Weasel*

The big stories that shape our lives — and Misty is one such story for me — are very often those that came to us in our childhood. These important formative stories can have any number of central characters, be they people, things, events, or animals. From reading and listening to hundreds of personal stories, I know that many of our first stories of deep importance have animal characters in them. Perhaps this is because as children we are naturally transfixed by animals and enchanted by them. We remember the circumstances surrounding our experiences with them. We remember them for their unusualness, for the sense of surprise they evoke, for the out-of-the-ordinary tickles or pokes they can inject into a day, a memory. We may remember nothing of the trip to Grandma's place, except for the moment when the hummingbird flew into the house and couldn't find its way out and Dad had to grab the cat and lock her in the bathroom for an hour.

And yet I do not believe that surprise or novelty is anywhere near the whole truth about the enduring strength of our first animal memories. It goes deeper than that. We remember these animal visitations as we would remember an encounter with an angel, a fairy sprite, or a wise and eccentric old relative. We remember them because they came to us to be remembered. They came with a message, with a host of messages most likely, and they will not be forgotten, most especially by the inspirited, mysterious, and still-free soul of a child.

In some of our earliest experiences, creatures come to us in beauty and gentleness, reminding us that these qualities live in the world, and in us. Some of them come on what seems to be a kamikaze mission, the lessons heart-pounding and the endings harsh. Some come to teach us something about ourselves, or about the world. No matter the reason, these animals come deliberately and earnestly, their soul-lives choreographed by the hand of the Holy One to cross paths with ours, and we remember them. This story-memory can become a catalyst for profound healing and reflection when we intentionally honor it, feel it, and then tell it, either in written or spoken words.

In a workshop I facilitated a few years back on writing about animals, I had the participants write about their earliest animal memory. The assignment was given on a late afternoon, and we were to all reconvene the next morning to read our pieces. Several of the class members were stumped. "I really don't have any strong memories. Really. We had an old dog. . . . No, I just can't quite remember." The challenge with this sort of exercise is that if you crack the door ever so slightly, that internal editor comes barging in. I have one of these internal critics inside of me, and I know how to get around him. "Just write," I said. "Trust me on this one."

And they did. When we gathered the next morning over coffee and fruit, everyone read, and everyone wept. Old farm dogs came to life on the page, scratching fleas and swan-diving into old swimming holes. A pet rabbit killed and passed off as a Thanksgiving Day turkey in a Depression household bore silent witness to childhood trusts betrayed. An ant farm was central to the life and future of one little girl. All the stories were unique, but the comments preceding the reading of each were identical: "I didn't know I had so much to tell. . . . I didn't know I still carried so much emotion about this. . . . I didn't remember anything until I sat down and started to write."

Our most meaningful stories are always those that address in some way these confoundingly human questions: Who am I? What should I do? Where did I come from? Where am I going? Childhood tales are an important place to begin our story-honoring journey because they often hold special keys to each of these questions. Yet until years of living have brewed in our bellies — perhaps until now — these stories may lie sleeping and forgotten in our hearts, waiting hopefully for us to take a long look back over our shoulder. Our first stories define where and who we have been, and they often set the stage of beliefs on which we will enact where we are going.

After *Animals as Teachers and Healers* was first published,

I received this story from Jacki, a contributor to that book: "For two days, my father cared for an injured wasp on our window sill. He brought it a jar-lid of fresh water each morning, pointed out to us kids the beautiful translucence of the wasp's wings, the delicacy of its legs. He was like a kid at Christmas.... By example, I learned that all life — All Life — was precious." Hers was not the first story, nor the last, to recount the primal importance of those first, early memories in the whittling of later beliefs about life.

The meaning we attach to our stories, conscious and unconscious, may propel, haunt, guide, confuse, or protect us in the decades to come. Animals come and go purposefully through our childhood, leaving tracks that still live and breathe within us. Misty continues to leave her tracks in my life. I did not realize until the writing of her memory how much of myself, my worldview, was sculpted in her coming and going. Just because a story came to us when we were small in size does not mean the story — the memory — is of small consequence. In fact, it usually reflects just the opposite. What we were and what we lived mixes its giant hand in our lives today and scrambles it all around. To move forward without tripping as much, take some time to look back over your shoulder and see the animal tracks following there, right behind you.

A Practice

I have no doubt that there is someone out there who is trying to get your attention. What memory is there, either staring you in the face like a dog at the dinner table or darting in and out of sight like a deer in the sage at the periphery of your vision?

Give yourself enough quiet time to awaken and invoke this wisp of your history. Perhaps a walk will loosen up the memory, or some sitting time beneath an old tree, or moments with a candle or special music.

When the story begins to tell itself to you, write it down. "In the beginning was the word," says the Bible, and the word was "with" God. "The word," in fact, gets first billing before God. Volumes are written on what "the word" actually means here. Personally, I believe "the word" in the biblical context defines the broadest possible scope of consciousness. And as a writer, I know that one of the most powerful tools for engaging consciousness is another kind of word — the kind we commit to paper.

Written words have a power that conjures the force of creation itself. I believe this has to do with the alchemy of mind and body. The mind gathers the words into ideas, and then the body goes to work with them. Our backs bend to the task, our shoulders rise, our hands move, and our thoughts are suddenly born and committed to the world of physical reality. Writing is one of the ways we can marry heaven (mind and spirit) and earth (body and soul). It is one of our most precious human gifts. Use it. Writing is a sacred act. Spirit and soul work through written words. You know this to be true — just remember a book or an article that grabbed you by the heart and held on fast, perhaps it holds onto you yet.

Whether you think you can write or not has nothing to do with the power of this process. Just do it! Write. And write as quickly as you can so that you keep at least one step ahead of your inner critic. Write until you know you are done. And you will know when you are done. It may be a page, it may be twenty pages, it may become a book.

Once you have taken the time you need to explore your story in writing (it may be hours, weeks, or years), share it in some way. If there is no one who you believe can receive it gently and respectfully, read it out loud in a private place. At first, this may feel really silly and you may squirm with discomfort at the sound of your own voice speaking to yourself, but if you follow the words that were given to you and give them voice, your story will deepen inside of you and its meanings will bloom. You will begin to touch the deeper truth of it all — you *are* your stories, and every character who populates those stories is a part of the living whole of you, as deserving of your awe and respect as your eyes, your hands, your heart. Listen, write, and tell.

Hermine's Children

When I was eight years old, my pet rat, Hermine, had seven fat babies. The rats were among my very first animal companions, and to my child's eyes, the bald, pink, maggot-like wonders were absolutely perfect and absolutely beautiful. They grew so quickly that they changed appearance dramatically between my first look at them each morning and my final goodnight to the brood at bedtime. In a matter of days, they transformed from worm-like blobs into hair balls the size of sewing thimbles.

When the rats were two weeks old with star-like eyes and fur as soft as pussy willows, I put them into a fold in my sweatshirt and carried them to the dining room for their first

taste of life beyond the rat cage. Gently, I deposited them onto
the dark cherry wood of our formal dining room table. Seven
small black bodies flattened against the dark wood. Seven pink
noses tested the air. Fourteen sparkling eyes were mirrored in
the gleaming veneer that was my mother's pride and joy. There
was a slight pause, a collective rat breath.

Suddenly — alarmingly — they dashed off in seven different directions, careening across the surface of the table like
spastic wind-up toys. They reached the four edges of the
table with lightning speed. But edges meant nothing to
infant rats with just fourteen days of living in their bellies.
Without pause, each tiny rat launched itself off the table and
catapulted like a pebble to the rug below. Horror stricken, I

crawled as fast as I could, gathering them up with my shaking fingers. Some were a bit dazed. Others never missed a beat and were charging off in whatever direction they had been headed before they became airborne. Still others curled in a ball beside a chair leg and refused to move.

Shamefaced and breathless, I quickly returned the babies to Hermine. I never told anyone about the rat debacle, keeping the hot guilt of it all to myself. I tried to put the memory of those airborne babies out of my mind as fast as I could, but in the days that followed, I could not stop myself from reliving the incident over and over in my mind. Something about the vision of those seven bodies leaping mindlessly and spread-legged into nothingness kept prodding at my brain. Like a taunting riddle, the discomfort of the memory would not release me. It seemed incomplete to me somehow, the story still unfinished.

My shame was great, but not as great as my curious, gnawing need, and so one morning about two weeks later when no one was in the house, I silently, secretly gathered up the seven rat babies and carried them furtively back to the dining room.

Now a month old, the youngsters filled my hands to overflowing. Their sleek bodies were strong and wiggly, and I knew the face and the feel of each cherished one of them. They were my dear, dear friends, and I was about to subject them — again — to possible harm. This time, I could not pretend I didn't know what I was doing. I knew it, I was red-faced with guilt about it, and yet I could not stop myself. In my shabby defense, all I can tell you is that the emotions that drove me seemed akin to a religious calling.

Time took on a trance-like, eerie quality when I opened my hands and watched seven young rats explode with curious delight onto the wide and gleaming expanse of cherry wood. Once again, seven pink noses tested the air. Seven smooth bodies pressed against the table's cool surface. Again, twenty-eight legs propelled the rats in seven different directions toward the edges of the table. I sucked in my breath and felt the hair on my arms raise in anticipatory alarm. Fast, fast they ran, noses twitching in rat ecstasy, tails held straight out behind them like ships' rudders. All together they reached the horizon of the table where the wood kissed the air. And all together they stopped.

North, south, east, and west, each rat paused as though rooted at the table's edge. Not one so much as extended a single rat toe into the abyss. I could feel their hesitation in my own body. I knew that they knew. Somehow, they had learned to recognize where the table stopped and the free fall began. Releasing my breath in a gasp, I could see nothing in the room but those rats on that table, nosing the air at the edge of their world, looking...looking. As though choreographed, they turned away from the edge and hurried back to the center of the table, where they met each other in a glorious burst of play. I gathered them back into my hands gently, humbly. The story was as complete as I needed it to be. Seven precious rats had taught me my first lesson about edges, about boundaries.

I spent much of my eighth summer in a tree. Our local park was home to an old pine that shaded a small playground. Although I quickly grew bored with the jungle gym and the swing set, that tree was something else entirely. I learned to climb up high, into the old pine's very throat, and to sit quietly on a particularly thick branch. Some days, I would bring along a bologna sandwich in a crumpled bag. Occasionally I would bring a book, but not often because books took my attention away from the tree itself. I listened to the sounds of the tree, all rustle and creak, bird-chirp and groan. But I came to know the tree by its edges. I knew the secret creases in the bark where my fingers needed to grip so that I could pull myself up to a firm foothold. I knew the exact line of hard soil where the tree trunk began and the upswell of roots ended. I knew the precise thickness of each of the pine arms: which were strong enough to hold me, and which would drop me to the ground. I knew also, and with great clarity, the differentiating line between the rough, scabby bark and the smoothness of my well-worn jeans pressed up against it as I sat, still, for hours.

The rats grew up and grew old, and as the years passed, I became too cool to sit in trees. Somewhere along the way, I forgot those first, clean lessons about edges and boundaries. I began prizing that endless expanse of veneer, the shimmering reflection of myself in the deep polish, and the rush of that seductive plunge into thin air.

My mother was never able to teach me about the value of healthy boundaries, or about the edges that define clearly and gently the shape of things. She and her twin brother had been raised by her grandparents in Germany. Her own parents — Oma and Opa to us — left my mom and her infant brother to seek a better life in America. Evidently, the life they found was so enjoyable that they simply "forgot" to send for the children. Oma loved to dance, and there was plenty of dancing to be done in New York City for a two-income couple with no children.

Only the threat of war in Europe fourteen years later would close the physical distance between my mother and her parents. Oma and Opa at last sent for the twins, afraid that if they didn't act then, something terrible might happen to their now-teenage children an ocean away. Mom tells me that the morning before they boarded the boat for America, she and her brother crept silently away before dawn to climb a lookout tower above their cobble-stoned village and watch the sun rise up, pink and sweet, over the streets of Bayreuth. In that town, at the Wagner Opera House, they had listened together to the impassioned speeches of Adolf Hitler and had worn proudly, innocently, the swastika armbands of the Hitler Youth.

Soon after they reached America, the war began. Before it was all over, my mother's beloved grandparents in Bayreuth were dead. Her brother, lying about his age, joined the Air Force to escape the terrible fighting at home that comes when parents try and assert themselves over foreign, un-known teenage children. Mom was left alone then to try and solve the riddle of parents who leave their children in another land and go dancing instead.

Opa died much too young, of a heart attack that took him in his sleep. For all the years until her death at ninety-three, Oma never tried to mend the tear between her and my mother. The betrayal hung between them for decades like mustard gas. To this day, my mother wants no part of sepa-rateness. In her world, edges and boundaries mark the bleak and sad borders between love and abandonment.

One winter evening on the near side of my thirties, I sat with a lover in the nervous silence of a psychologist's office. The counselor, a gorgeous, wild-haired woman, gave us two pieces of chalk and told us to sit on the floor and draw circles around ourselves. These circles were to symbolically represent us. I took up the shard of chalk and drew a bold mark on the blue carpet. My circle extended about a foot out from my body and I sat loose and comfortable in its center.

Then Michael took the chalk, scooted across the carpet toward me, and — how else can I say this? — launched himself like a tiny rat off the dining room table. His circle extended out in a wide arc that overlapped the edges of mine. As the white chalk line moved across the private frontier of my circle, my shoulders sucked up to the bottoms of my ears. My knees sank into my chest, and my neck into my spine. Inches vanished from my height. I recoiled away from the invading chalk as if it were a pile of steaming cat droppings.

"This is the part of me that is closest to Susan," Michael said as he pointed lovingly to the four inches of overlap that joined us together. The counselor turned to me. "What does this mean to you, Susan?" My answer came roaring out, my voice too loud, too furious. I aimed an accusing finger at the spot. "That's the war zone. It's every fight…" I hunted quickly for the right words: "It's our sickest part." I thrust my arm forward, and as fast as my hand could rub, I wiped Michael out from my circle. Grabbing for the stump of chalk, I drew the edges of our circles to press together tentatively, like two thin lips. My belly ceased its death grip. "This feels better to me."

Smothered by a family dynamic that mistook absorption for love, I had somehow retained enough of myself to be repelled by invasion. That night, the counselor confirmed for both of us that the rings gently touching along their edges represented the healthier picture of intimacy, of boundaries defended and respected. I learned, again, that edges are valuable, defensible. That is, I learned once again what I'd been shown at eight by a cluster of innocent rodents.

Fifteen years ago, I found a large sore underneath my tongue. A pathology report called it, rather poetically I thought, "sheets and nests" of cancer. Battling it led me to a new edge I had never explored. At thirty-seven, I plunged off the edge of my own table, thudded against death, and landed dazed in a heap after the free fall. In no uncertain terms, illness framed the edges of my life. Cancer was the exact separating ground between root and trunk. It was the rim of another circle, pressed like thin lips against the rim of mine. Marked by such clear and fragile boundaries, my life became starkly visible and achingly precious.

To feel the edges between life and death, I needed only to touch the raw threads of a hundred stitches etched like train tracks from my left ear to my collar bone. During that sacred and terrifying time, other edges butted up against me. They were not table tops or trees or chalk marks on the floor. They were lab charts and hospital beds. They were sales packets cruelly sent to me, unsolicited, by local cemeteries and funeral parlors.

Surgeries and fear sharpened my edges even further. Slowly, I came to know where my own fear ended and the fear of those who loved me began. I learned to balance clumsily along the harrowing edge between wanting to live forever and being willing to let everything and everyone go completely. I promised myself that my family, my friends, and my medical team wouldn't get past me at the edge of my life without at least pressing their circle up against mine. And most of them didn't.

I don't know if that sweet old tree still stands in the park I used to visit. I know that the rats, babies and all, are long gone to whatever heaven welcomes animal saints. The cancer is fifteen years gone — gone for good, I believe. And I am still here, finally owning what I'd learned from a passel of inquisitive rats: It is important to honor the edges of things.

Stigmatized Relations

VARMINTS, VERMIN, AND STEREOTYPING

"You dirty rat!"

— Any gangster to another

You would think that I would follow Hermine's story with a reflection on personal boundaries. But I am nudged firmly to go elsewhere. It is Hermine's ratness that calls to me and the fact that some of my greatest teachers and healers were what we collectively refer to as "vermin." Hermine's memory links me back to another story from another time, one that was also wrapped in a rodent face.

Thousands of feet above the ground, whizzing through the air at speeds human bodies are not meant to go, I fumbled for a magazine in the seatback in front of me and found a *Sky Mall* catalog, and behind that, a fat and glossy publication with a prairie dog on the cover. The face of the large rodent with the happy eyes brought a smile to my lips. Thanks to Hermine and her children, I have a deep affinity for the face and form of rodents, all kinds of rodents. The prairie dog on the magazine cover was sitting up with his tiny hands curled into curious fists, and his nose pointed to the sky. I expected the title of the magazine to be some kind of nature thing and was surprised to see the words "Varmint Hunter" across the top. I did a double take, even turning the

magazine over to look at the back cover, which was a photo
montage of different kinds of ammunition. At first, I
thought it was some sort of a *National Lampoon*–styled
satire, but I was wrong. Inside were advertisements for guns
and bullets specifically created for blasting to oblivion a
whole series of small creatures that our culture has defined as
varmints. These include animals and birds who we have
decided bother us in some way. Perhaps they dig holes, eat
plants we treasure, snitch corn, topple garbage cans, hang
out at landfills, steal chickens or cats, or are just plain fun to
shoot. The hunters in the magazine's photos wore camou-
flage gear, night goggles, and ammunition belts, looking like
soldiers in the war on terrorism.

I kept the magazine for years as a pictorial and editorial
record of just how insane humans can be — and how ridiculous grown men can look and behave. It was lost in one of
my many moves, and I decided not to replace it. God forbid
that I should ever contribute a cent to such stupidity.

How do we convince all that is humane in us that it is
okay to kill helpless living beings, creatures who share our
same needs for food and shelter? It's not easy; we have to flip
a switch in our heads that shuts off our soul. Humankind has
found this switch in words. We assign words and labels to
lives we choose to take for no good reason, words that make
these lives worth far less than ours and seemingly deserving
of their ill fate at our hands. In this way, we feel little or no
shame or remorse at their deaths.

One currently popular word we use to describe this
shameful practice is "demonizing." This is a fine, slicing
word that offers a visceral sense of the process. We use this

term to describe what we do to larger animals and to populations of people we seek to kill. For instance, we demonize wolves and terrorists and, until very recently, native Americans. "Demonizing" is the heaviest word, the most extreme and reckless form of this practice of anesthetizing the human soul. There is another word, however, that is perhaps more dangerous because it is subtle and insidious, much less raw and in-your-face. It is a germinating word that culminates in the slaughter of animals and people, places and spirit. The word is "stereotyping." We all do it. We are enculturated to the process from birth, and in many ways, it seems innocent enough.

It *seems* innocent. Stereotyping starts so small, and it leans a bit on humor and amusement to get the soul yawning and its eyelids a bit droopy. So often, we begin stereotyping with animals. Here is what I have been told by books, movies, school, teachers, and peers about certain vilified or mocked animals, and what I know to be true from a life of exploring animals as my relations:

Culture and Western religion tell me that snakes are sinister. I can tell you from a lifetime of keeping snakes, especially when I was a child, that they are not. I knew them to be gentle, watchful, peaceful, and always grinning from ear to ear. Their mouths are perpetually curved into a lazy smile. Human faces could use a bit of that same geography.

Young voices on the playground at school tell me that chickens are cowards — as in the phrase, "So-and-so is a chicken." This is ludicrous folly. Pound for pound, chickens are the Davids of the Goliath legend. They will sacrifice their lives for their families in an instant. In my memory, I hold the image of a dead rooster, lying in front of his flock of ten hens. A dog had slaughtered them all, but the rooster's feathers were everywhere, and his spur marks tracked across the face and ears of the dog in bloody lines. The rooster had fought a 104-pound malamute to his death. Although his body was nearly in pieces when we found him, I have no doubt his courage remained intact to the very end.

I don't know who ever coined the phrase "eats like a bird" to describe a timid appetite. Birds are not the dainty Victorians of the epicurean world. They eat like sharks and consume an enormous amount of food in comparison to their body weight. Have you never pondered that feeding frenzy at the bird feeders? If you were to put that morning ritual to the background music of *Jaws,* you might have a more true picture of birds and appetites.

Children's literature and all popular media tell me that rabbits are gentle, timid creatures, and that this is the whole of the matter. Having had a house rabbit for many years, I can assure you that bunnies also harbor a side that is neither gentle nor timid. While I can still go all goo-goo at the photo of a baby bunny in tall spring grass, I also have memories of bunnies charging workshop participants, with teeth out, growling like bulldogs. I remember my own rabbit chasing me across my dining room floor in her frisky teens, trying to sink her teeth into my foot. These are not the pictures we see in animal calendars. Rabbits are symbolically linked to fear in certain traditions, and I can attest to that, having run in fear from more than one of them. Rabbits themselves do not run from fear. They run because they can. They run because they are faster than you. Their teeth are very long,

and their growl is as hair-raising as the legendary High-
lander's yell. Rabbits are a lot more than just a sweet face.

The dirtiness of pigs is taken as a fact throughout our
culture. But pigs are not dirty. They far prefer a clean envi-
ronment. Pigs use mud as we use zinc ointment — it is a
good sunscreen and skin protector. In a study done many
years ago, pigs were offered a mud wallow, or a shower and
shade. The pigs chose the showers and the shade every time.
A wild boar once came charging at me out of the brush on a
remote tropical island. While I was too terrified to notice
much else, I did notice that he was not dirty. He was sleek
and fast and shiny black, and he chased me up a coconut
palm with great efficiency. While it is true that pigs do get
vocal over their food, I have relatives who make far worse
sounds over a picnic table.

While Western culture stereotypes certain animals as
"less than," it also has a penchant for elevating others to a
level of false grandiosity. I learned as a child that eagles and
lions are brave and noble. In pictures and on television, I
never saw images of them fleeing in fear, rolling in mud,
belching, or huddling. And yet what animal does not have its
very own sense of pride and nobility if we just take the time
to look closely and with an open heart? Doesn't your cat take
over her favorite chair with a certain level of authority? Isn't
the dove cooing and bobbing over his mate the very epitome
of pride? Lions and eagles should not have to shoulder that
pride and nobility burden all the time, and in real life, they
don't. I once watched an eagle dive for a trout in the Snake
River. I don't know how large the fish was, but the eagle had
clearly overestimated his abilities. He grabbed the fish with

his talons, and I watched, stunned, as the trout pulled him underwater and kept going. The eagle surfaced a ways downstream, flapping and sputtering his way to shore. When he arrived, I can tell you he didn't look proud. He looked like a wet sack with big yellow feet.

A rat is a rat is a rat. It is not "vermin," nor is it simply a larger version of the Pied Piper's legions. Some rats are like Hermine — soft, kind-eyed, maternal. Some rats are... well, you need to experience ratness for yourself.

Stereotypes are dangerous, and sometimes they are dangerously grandiose. We may not recognize the profound wisdom of a rat because the collective box we have put rats in is labeled "dirty, diseased, vicious, and creepy." And by the same token, we may take as gospel the twisted logic that comes out of the mouth of a president because we have a collective belief that presidents are honorable, smart, and dedicated to the public good. I am grateful that in a moment of childish brilliance, I heeded the wisdom of seven airborne infant rodents. Experience — not blind assumption or acceptance — is the mother of all teachers, and I thank Hermine's children for delivering to me my very own, personalized state-of-the-interior-union address.

A Practice

Let's go outside again — anywhere, country or city. Find a place that calls to you, or a place that repels you, and take a journal along. Ask the power of nature for her help with this exercise. The asking is important — it is like putting on sneakers before you start walking the sharp stone beds of tide pools: You'll get farther and see more. Ask nature out loud for lessons that will deepen your understanding about stereotypes.

As you walk, make a list of things that capture your attention in some way, positive or negative. It can be anything, the green grass on a country path, the gray pigeons in the city, the cold, the wind. Discount nothing. Put to bed the voice that says, "Gee, did I really notice this, or was I making myself notice it?" Of the thousands of things that could claim your attention as you walk, trust that nature is conspiring to bring to your attention only the things you need to see for your own unique exploration of stereotyping. This may be the hardest part of the exercise for you — it often is for me: trust.

Before you conclude your stroll, thank the wisdom of nature for helping you. Leave a gift of gratitude — a song, a prayer, seeds, appreciation.

At home, sit down with your list of attention-getters and select maybe two or three items. For each one, write down every association you can think of — those things you have been told, have read, have imagined, or have experienced yourself. Make your lists for each item as thorough as possible. Do not edit yourself. Resist the urge to strike a word or phrase from your list because it sounds small-minded or not very spiritual, or because it sounds too lofty or too trite.

When you feel your listings are as complete as you can make them, make yourself a cup of tea or coffee and then go back over each list, circling every association you have written down that does not come from your own personal experience. If you have lots of circles on your page, great: You have prime fodder for exploring the roots of stereotyping. Being both gentle and honest with yourself, can you distinguish where you have subjugated your own experience to the opinions and attitudes of others? Or where you have not bothered to explore your own experience with something because your beliefs have already been cemented by the convictions of others?

For example, I admit I am programmed very negatively about cities, and in part, this is because my small community enforces my own prejudices about crowded spaces. I listen as those around me lambaste the dirtiness, danger, congestion, traffic, and lack of community in cities, and I nod my head numbly and self-righteously, glad to be on the same wavelength with my neighbors and acquaintances. Yet my own experience of cities is also of beautiful lights glittering at night, congenial folks bumping elbows in line for a ballet, stores with more than one model of toaster. If I listen to the group consensus alone, I can find myself drowning out my own experience and miss the gifts cities have to offer.

It can be wonderfully exhilarating to let go of the opinions of the collective and trust — or create — our own experiences. In this lies the dismantling and healing of stereotypes of all kinds, and the opening of our hearts to greater union.

The Goddess and the Chicken

Last winter, I had a powerful dream about the Great Goddess, filled with symbols and pictographs. In this dream, I was to retrieve and "keep safe from all harm the sacred mummy" of the Great Goddess, which had been hidden for thousands of years. I plucked the Goddess's burial chamber from the back ledge of a darkened, freshly excavated cave, and when I carried it out into the light, I discovered that what I had in my hand was a swallow's mud nest. The tiny desiccated Goddess mummy inside was about the size of a child's fist, wrapped in a shroud of stained, ancient linen.

I'd been reading about the Goddess and the Feminine with great interest for over a year, devouring fascinating

books that document the history of Goddess spirituality and celebrate this ancient, feminine consciousness that is reblossoming now on Earth. Transpersonal psychologist Marion Woodman[1] defines this feminine energy as "bringing the wisdom in nature to consciousness." How could I not be enchanted with the return of feminine consciousness if it would herald a return to nature-centered thinking?

Then came my dream of the nest coffin, and the shriveled holy figure that I cupped with wonder in my hands. In my dream, the only part of the mummy that time had exposed were two tiny twig-like legs, which sported little silver filagree high-heeled pumps on pea-sized feet. It was not until I woke up that I recalled that the legs looked very much like bird legs.

This bird figure came as no surprise to me. In my own interior vision, I have always modeled my own image of the Goddess after the most courageous, maternal, no-nonsense, earthy, sensuous spirits I know — chickens. While some would lean toward statues of the Black Madonna or Baubo, or a vision of full and overflowing wombs, I stick to chickens. They are for me "the Deep Feminine" in body and in spirit.

The more potent and profound the archetype, the more I rely on animals to model it for me. Man-made gods and goddesses are heavily laden with the confounding baggage of human craziness, and I have always found psychospiritual models in animal form to be less conflicted. Many years ago, I saw God appear in my mind's eye as a Canada goose. I was surprised at this image when it came, but when I reflected on the wonder of Bird as winged mediator between heaven and Earth, the goose made perfect sense. So, then, does the Goddess as Chicken — the most grounded, practical, abundant bird on Earth.

My Goddess instruction by chickens began when I was a toddler. In the Catskill Mountains of New York, my Gypsy grandmother kept a poultry farm. I have photos of myself and my brother as infants, lying on old blankets outside of the white, 100-year-old clapboard farmhouse. We spent summers there until I was three, when we all moved out West. Most photos taken of me in those early years show me carrying some sort of small animal around, mostly puppies with their tails dragging between my chunky, baby legs.

Even though I have pictures to remind me, I don't recall any of the animals on the farm — the cows, the ducks, the dogs, the barn cats, the hawks, the skunks — except for the chickens. They completely mesmerized me. We ate them nearly every day, but I was too small to associate the fried thing on my plate with the feathery creatures strutting in the yard. I don't even have to close my eyes to see them in my mind — big, multicolored, round, deliberate. The hens stood as tall as my chest, the roosters much taller than that.

More than anything in my life, I wanted to hug the chickens, which was utterly absurd because I probably could not have gotten my stubby arms all the way around one of them. I spent hours stumbling after them, however, calling out my own version of "Here, chick-chick-chick." Of course, they never came. They must have seen me as some crazed naked chicken myself, one who couldn't even manage a decent "cluck." Grandma knew the robust hens and roosters were smart and swift, so she let me run off my energy every day in my vain attempts at chicken communion. They frustrated the diapers off me. I could not even get in a fleeting pet, a stroke of glistening feathers. They would parade around me in a congenial and collected bunch, always just out of reach.

"Brruck...burrruck...bucck...buk," the group muttered back and forth when they saw me at a distance. They never seemed to stop talking among themselves, and the sound was such a comforting one, so very chatty and personable. They spent their days scratching earnestly at places in the dirt and strutting and conversing. I saw them take dust baths where they had clawed the soil to a particularly fine silt, and I believed what my Grandma said about dust baths being good, until I took one myself.

My favorite time of the day was afternoon, when Grandma would let me go with her to gather eggs. Grandma was dark-skinned and black-eyed, with raven hair as glossy as feathers. She stood as proud in her worn house dresses and stained aprons as those chickens. She was no-nonsense, too, thick in the hip and belly, and her eyes missed nothing. In the chicken house, we slipped into our own world, a dusty, sun-shafted place of ripe smells and noises that felt inclusive, mothering, secret, and as soft as my grandmother's enormous, pendulous breasts.

The nest boxes were up high out of my reach, and I sometimes came face to belly with a chicken nestled in the hay. The hen would look down at me with copper eyes and mutter a soft "grrruck...grrruckkkk," cocking her narrow head sideways, confident that Grandma would keep her safe from me. We heard them speak in that same soft chant at night if we were called out to the hen house for some reason or another. It sounded as sweet and reassuring as a lullaby. I did not know that they were singing for their children, who floated peacefully and expectantly in their yolk-ocean eggs. Grandma always let some hens hatch out clutches of chicks. Because the hens ranged free, their life spans were not long, so Grandma had a steady need for up-and-comers.

Each day I was warned not to stick my hand up into the nest boxes. If there was an egg there, Grandma would find it and hand it to me, and I'd put it in a pail. Sometimes I reached up anyhow, and a hen would scream in outrage and peck at my hand with a beak like a nail gun, while the roosters sounded a startled alarm outside. The pecks hurt enough to bawl, but I knew that if I did, Grandma's sympathies would be with the offended chicken.

If you can imagine my frustration at not being able to hug the chickens, then multiply that by ten when it came to the chicks. I was no more effective in grabbing them than I was their parents. The exquisite little puffballs whose very sight made my palms tingle would vanish like a school of tiny fish into the protective sea of hens. I knew the chickens were totally and justifiably disgusted with me for trying to kidnap their children, because they cursed me in a very accusatory tone whenever I would try to sneak up on them while pretending to be very preoccupied by clouds. I think it was one of my first experiences of shame, but it didn't stop me.

In the rare moments when I would somehow get too close to the yard convention of hens, one would bellow out a blaring "CLUCK! CLUCK!!" and suddenly, all the hens would take it up, the roosters would bellow and flap, and the chicks would shriek and race for cover under boards or under their mothers. Mass chaos would overcome the whole lot of them, and I'd run away. They had me pegged. It worked every time.

Years passed, and Grandma died. I don't know who got the farm. Or the chickens. But when my then-husband Lee and I closed the deal on our first home in Oregon — a small farm with a barn — I had chickens on the brain before the ink was dry on the paper. A very dilapidated greenhouse made from fiberglass panels and old boards stood out back in view of the kitchen window, and Lee was in favor of tearing it down. It would have probably been the better choice from an aesthetic point of view, but I coaxed him into the idea of fresh eggs and the delight of being woken up by a real rooster.

We moved into the farmhouse in December, and in February I raced to the feed store the day they got in their first batch of spring chicks. I was besotted with delight at the prospect of being a chicken mother, not realizing that over the next few years, they would be mothering me in ways I could not have imagined then.

Burn's Feedstore prided itself on its fowl collection. You could get any manner of feathered barnyard creatures there, from paired goslings to bee-sized baby quail, to wildly colored bantam chickens and laying pullets. The poultry room was warm and humid, each wooden box of babies bedded in clean, aromatic shavings and heated with a soft, red lamp. I loved to go there and sit. Like other people would visit a library just to relax and enjoy the literary ambience, I would go to Burn's poultry room to soak in the tart smells of pine shavings and chicken poop, the sound of hundreds of voices peeping on a high and ear-sweet tonal scale, and the tender sight of the birds themselves: yellow, black, red, striped, spotted, fluffy as powder puffs.

On that damp, chilly day in February I brought home a small box of them, naming them all before we even got home. Of that first family flock, I remember Ozzie and Harriet, the two red Cochin Bantams; Maggie, Maybell, Maud, and Mary, the barred Rock pullets; Ink and Silkie, the two black Silkie Bantams; and finally, two bearded Belgian quail, who were not yet quail but very tiny banty chicks who would grow tufted "beards" on their faces if they survived infancy.

The chicks lived at first near the kitchen stove, in a cardboard box that grew in size as they did. I suspended a heat lamp above their box with a wire twisty tie, adjusting it by "feel." If the chicks sprawled out, panting, on the perimeters of the light, I raised the lamp. If they gathered beneath it and made a certain contented sound in their throats, I knew it was "just right." Our whole family — human and animal — spent hours at that box. Reilly, the owner of Burn's Feedstore, told me that my cats would not bother the infant chicks — something about chickens at that very tender age would not attract predatory attention — and miraculously, he was right. Arrow, my dog, and the cats — Bear, Evinrude, and Flora — watched the chicks like a television show, but they never showed any desire to chase or eat them.

With luck and with my near-obsessive care, they grew. Not a single chick died. They went from gangly, mini-dinosaur-looking things to plump, sleek, beautiful birds. Their voices matured into the low, chatty singsong music of contented hens. We had two roosters in the group — Ozzie (a lucky guess of a name on my part) and one of the Belgian quails. One day, about six months after I brought them home, I found a pearl-colored egg resting on a gold bed of straw in the chicken coup. More followed — some big, some tiny as pigeon eggs, in colors ranging from white to speckled brown. Suddenly, each day included my own personal Easter egg hunt.

Summer green melted into the clear gold of autumn. Winter came, then spring. Then winter and spring again. Coyotes visited our fenced yard, and a raccoon, and hawks. The neighbor's border collie from around the corner snuck into our yard for a week before we discovered him hurrying through a tunnel in the blackberry bushes with Maybell limp in his mouth. He had taken a chicken each time. A bathtub set up as a watering trough for the donkeys became Ozzie's watery grave one sad afternoon. But generations of chicks were born in the coop, and some in the hayloft of the barn. By our third year on the farm, the chickens numbered into the twenties. Of the original chicken family raised in our kitchen, these remained: Harriet the red Cochin, Silkie the black lady, and the bearded Belgian and her husband.

The chicken coop was a world of ever-increasing wonder to me, no longer a dilapidated fiberglass shed, but a feathered temple of sorts. I went daily to the coop not so much to gather garden fertilizer and eggs as to enter a nonordinary state of consciousness. The sounds and smells would take me instantly back to Grandma's farm. In the afternoon light of swirling dust motes, I could feel the ghost of her great arms surround me, pulling me against a bosom as soft as goose down, as big as a pillow. The chicken coop was the best place in the world to be mothered — in the most expansive sense of that word — not just by a childhood remembrance, but by the chickens themselves.

In the coop, the Goddess spoke regularly. Here is one of the many, many truths she told from the chickens' lips: The Mother is always larger than any of her earthly containers, but sometimes smaller is grander — like a diamond compressed from coal.

The most diminutive representative of the Goddess in our flock was, for years, the bearded Belgian quail. True to the promise on the description card over her wooden bin at

Burn's, she did sprout a fuzzy "beard" when she grew her adult plumage. It looked very peculiar, this beard. Imagine Groucho Marks's moustache in brown and white speckles, sprouting from both sides of his nose rather than from beneath it, and you've got a fair idea of the Belgian.

In coloring, she was a wild girl, mottled coffee-colored and pewter and sleek like a hawk, with a head just as streamlined except for that beard. She was less than half the size of our regular banties, which were about a third the size of the laying hens. In my palm, she perched like a quiet dove, her soft cluck befitting her size. Timid when she was a tiny chick, the Belgian outgrew her shy caution and became as friendly as a little dog. She would follow me about the yard, eager to see what I was into in the garden, always happy to be gathered up and stroked and to have that bristly beard scritched.

When her Belgian rooster husband vanished into thin air one day, she joined the rest of the flock and suffered the amorous attentions of roosters three times her size with little complaint. It was when the drake duck turned his attentions on her that she demonstrated the enormity of her indignation. Male ducks have a penis of shocking orange that spirals like a corkscrew and is about as long. When excited, they grab their intended by the feathers on the head, mount up, and then peck incessantly on their partner's heads until the union is over or they fall off, whichever happens first. We have had many ducks, but none like this particular drake. His libido was never dormant, and before long, nearly all the ducks and all the chickens in the yard were bald. But the Belgian was one to protest. If she could not run fast enough to get away from him, which she most often did, she would attack him with her beak and wings until his ardor cooled. She kept her dignity at all times, and her head feathers and her beard, too.

Of all our hens, the Belgian was the most serious about her brooding, hardly ever leaving her nest of eggs and starting a new clutch as soon as each batch of babies was feathered. I lost count of her offspring. Her clutches were large, and it was not unusual to see her strutting around the yard with a huge crowd of chicks, many adopted from hens who were overworked or distracted with their own brood, or who had died suddenly. She was fiercely protective; no dog was safe in her range. I once saw her flip up onto her back and strike her feet out at a hawk while her young chicks dispersed like sparks.

One spring evening, she failed to show up at the coop. Because the lives of free-ranging chickens can be so brief, I tried very hard not to have "favorites," as it seemed my favorites never lasted very long. But of course, that was impossible. The Belgian was as dear to me as a beloved puppy. When she showed up at the barn the next morning, I celebrated by giving her a secret meal of corn behind the llama manger.

I don't remember what was preoccupying me, but I didn't notice for quite some time that she began meeting me in the llama stall every morning. Not only did she meet me, but she did a little dance for me each morning, turning right, then left, then relaxing her wing tips and spinning for me in a slow, fluttering spiral. All the while, she would sing a soft "brrrrkkk...brrrkkk...brrrk." Touched by her display, I would stand and watch her until the dance was complete, at

which time she would strut under the fence rail toward the
hay bales, still calling to me, and that would be that.

How many obvious signs parade under our noses until
we see them, suddenly, finally, for the first time? How many
signs all lined up in a row do we never see because our minds
have left our bodies and are wafting about in space? The
dance, the song, the strut, the hay bales: The Belgian had
been trying to signal me for days, while my head waggled far
above her, lost in some personal clouds.

I was spilling grain into the llama manger one morning
when the signals finally appeared on my interior screen and I
first saw the dance for what it was. The Belgian was beckon-
ing me. Her dance continued around my ankles as I stepped
forward to meet her. She moved slowly toward the hay bales
behind the llama stall, her feet leaving tiny Y-shaped tracks in
the fine dust and leading me to a broken bale tumbled down
between the stall rails and a stack of firewood. As she strutted, she turned back to me, bobbing her head, urging me
along. She sang a soft song all the while, each "cluck" ending
in an up note. She turned then and reached forward with her
beak, her outstretched head and neck like a slim finger,
pointing.

There in the dark corner on a bed of old gray straw
rested the object of her delight and obvious pride: It was
a *nest*. Not an ordinary soup-bowl-sized affair with three
to a half-dozen eggs, but a veritable throne of eggs. She had
reached for a personal best. I knelt down in the dust and she
hurried to stand in front of me, bobbing, twirling, singing.
Her tiny black eyes met and held mine. It was all there: joy,
excitement, a secret shared, a dream awaited, a job well done,

an accomplishment of enormous proportions — all reflected in those eyes no bigger than grains of sand, set in a skull that housed a brain no bigger than my fingertip.

How could so much soul, so much mother, be housed in so small a package, I asked myself. Her presence beamed huge in her happiness, flooding the barn with another kind of light. I leaned forward and stroked her, and she dipped down beneath my hand and cooed. As I picked up and inspected each egg with a murmur of approval, she tiptoed onto the nest and touched her eggs with the tip of her beak, stroking them with the side of her bristly beard. There were sixteen in all — far, far too many for her to have incubated with her tiny body. The Belgian must have moved from one end of the nest to the other, hour to hour, to try and keep them all warm and growing. It was a miracle, or a testimony to her ferocity, that no predators had invaded her isolated and vulnerable nursery.

I was stunned at her accomplishment, her determination, and humbled that she so obviously wanted to share her maternal treasures with me, as though I — childless all my life — could relate to the mystery of birth through her abundant giving. And in my own Goddess way, I could. I'd given birth to the vision of the chicken coop, to the idea of my flock, and to stories and ideas and dreams, each a pearlescent egg of sorts to be warmed, rolled, tended, and hatched at the right time.

In respect for her mother-of-the-world dream, I placed the Belgian and her nest into a huge kennel fitted with food and water so that she and her brood would be safe from harm as she eased into the final stages of hatching her small nation of eggs. She appreciated it, I could tell. Six days later, nine chicks the size of peanuts clustered beneath her, a huge brood for a dove-sized bird. The remaining eggs I took into the pasture out back. Their nutrients would perhaps be life for someone else, and the unhatched chicks might become, through their molecular absorption, foxes, weasels, soil, or mice. The nine remaining chicks thrived, loved to life by a tiny and powerful Goddess.

The Belgian's favorite chicken companion was the one remaining black Silkie Bantam. Twice, the two hens sat side-by-side on the same nest of eggs and raised the clutch of chicks together. The Silkie was also one of my "beloved" chickens — that is, the ones who seemed tragically destined to short lives. It was not just the Silkie's life, but the events that occurred after she lost it, that taught me yet another of the deep mysteries of the Goddess and of mothering.

Silkie was an odd-looking bird, like a long-haired black guinea pig with a beak. Because of my negligence, her most recent clutch of chicks had been made vulnerable to a raccoon visit, and by the following morning, only one nut-sized, red baby had survived the intrusion. Silkie tended that baby with special attention, her maternal energies all poured into that precious remaining "one." A week later, just as the bearded Belgian was beginning to parade her crowd of nine chicks around the yard, I watched in horror as Silkie was snatched out of the yard by a coyote, the whole incident over in seconds.

Silkie never had time to make a sound. But her chick did. From the moment her mother was carried off, flapping but silent, she broke the stillness with a piercing cry that was to continue for hours. Silkie's youngster had just begun to feather out and was still far to young to fend for herself. She was also far too fast to be captured by anything less agile than a coyote, and I spent most of my remaining day trying to sneak up on her with a butterfly net, with absolutely no success. By afternoon, she quieted and was seemingly contented in the company of the main flock, pecking at bugs, dozing in the sun. I noticed with interest that she seemed to follow the gray Silkie rooster around the yard. The rooster looked much like the chick's mother — a slightly larger and pewter-colored version of a guinea pig with a beak. My neighbor, a veterinarian whose own chicken flock was penned up, told me that her rooster routinely killed small chicks. But this gray fellow seemed fine with the company of the little red one.

That evening, the hatchling's plaintive caterwauling began again after she followed the flock into the hen house and watched all the chickens — rooster included — fly into the rafters for the night. Silkie had been sleeping on the floor of the coop, and she would have remained there until her chick was able to flutter into the safety of the rafters with her. But now the orphaned chick raced in confused terror around the vacant flooring of the coop, crying piteously as twenty-something chickens clucked out to her in alarm.

In the confines of the coop, I was at last able to grab the chick, and on a hunch, I reached up and placed her on a rafter close to the rooster. Instantly, she scuttled over to him and pressed against his wing. My eyebrows raised when he lifted up his bottom and invited her to creep between his legs. She accepted with a soft chirp, and he settled down with a hen-like wiggle, enveloping the red chick in the sustaining warmth of his belly feathers. I had never seen a rooster do this. I would never see it again. But I saw it and honored it then.

By next morning, he had taken over care of the red chick fully. I watched him patrol the yard, stopping to point his beak and cackle for the chick. As he clucked in encouragement, she would grab up whatever food he had found for her. I had seen him do this for his hens, as his hens did for their chicks. He was the perfect mother to the red hatchling, and remained so until she became a mother herself the following spring.

I am a bit ashamed to admit that I had expected far less of that rooster, simply because he was a rooster — a guy. Yet that fuzzy, gray chicken gave me pause. A lot of pause. I asked myself, How could so much mother be housed in the body of a father? The Goddess chuckled. And sometimes she clucked, and sometimes she crowed.

Nonsexual Relations

MASCULINE, FEMININE, AND GENDER

*The ways of the feminine have traditionally honored
all life as sacred, have emphasized receptive states of being
rather than expressive states of doing, have reflected the inter-
connectedness of all life, and have not allowed the community
to be forgotten in the pursuit of individual achievement.*

— Hilary Hart, *The Unknown She*

Here is a condensed version of what I have read over many years about feminine and masculine energy archetypes: The feminine is receptive, communal, internally oriented, instinctual, earthy, moist, wild, creative, birthing, nurturing; the Mother, the Maiden, the Hag, and the Goddess. The masculine energy is the Warrior, the King, the Father, God — dry, hot, externally oriented, protective, achieving, guarding, thinking.

While I agree with the characterizations of these two arche-typal polarities — that in the universe there is an outward-thrusting force and an inward, receptive force that invites it, thus founding the creative tension of the middle ground — I have no idea who assigned the words to these two energies that affiliated each with a gender. If I could find that person now, I would throttle him. I would throttle him because of all the baggage and pain and confusion I have carried in my own life about what constitutes a manly man, or a feminine female. If I were queen for a day, I would change the terms "masculine" and "feminine" to a pairing less supercharged and loaded, to something like "Frit and Frat."

Chickens have a secret, and they will tell it to you if you listen. They speak it on behalf of every other animal in the world who knows the same thing: The feminine archetype has little to do with being female. The masculine is not about being a male. These qualities of thrusting and receiving have very little to do with sex and gender, the procreative particulars of thrusting and receiving notwithstanding. In a successful, well-rounded life, we all thrust, we all receive, we all mother, we all protect. We apply each as it is needed. Balance is the goal, and the lack of that archetypical balance has polarized the world into a global patriarchy where the Goddess feminine is respected and valued just about as much as a chicken.

A rooster can mother. A hen can protect. A male dog will try to nurse puppies; a female dog will die for them. The definitions of male behaviors and female behaviors, across species borders, are not unilaterally matched with those virtues and energies we call "masculine" and "feminine."

How much misery in your personal and cultural life have you experienced because of the terrible mix-up this language has spawned? Think of the phrases "bitchy, castrating women," "feminine, sissy men," "pushy broads," and "nerdy guys." How many good, strong qualities of assertion or tenderness do we dismiss simply because they appear in the "wrong" gender package?

Chickens show us differently. A creature we call simple because it has a brain the size of a pea and because it can poop, have sex, and make babies all out of the same orifice (which to me signifies a rather elegant, advanced state of streamlined development) can exhibit more dignity than some humans when it comes to just doing what it takes in life, whether the doing requires mothering or fathering, gentleness or ferocity. Although I would like to believe I am truly open-minded in all things, the truth is that I, too, have been indoctrinated to equate the Goddess with mothering, mothering with the archetypal feminine, and the feminine with females. Now, can't you just see my Silkie rooster shaking his head at me and saying, "Ahem"?

A Practice

Find some time alone outside. If you are tempted to look out a window and let your view substitute for being outside, try this activity both ways. I find that even a pane of glass disrupts the flow of nature's wordless message to me. Even just stepping out your door and sitting in your yard or on a small balcony will enrich this exercise. It is the difference between phone contact or holding hands with a loved one. Which would you choose? Nature chooses the hand-holding option.

Seek a place that calls to you, and when you have found it, ask the place for its consent for you to visit with it. Mothers are right when they tell their children to say "please" and "thank you." In asking nature and her elements for consent, you are in essence saying "please" to the biggest Mother you will ever meet in this lifetime. Gaining permission for your visit simply means that you feel welcomed and safe in this place.

After you have gained permission, ask for nature's help as

you reflect upon the words "masculine" and "feminine." Spend time with these two powerful words, time that will reflect the importance of these archetypes to our lives and our world. Ask the God to hold hands with the Goddess for a while, and the rooster to stand a moment beside the hen.

Now consider this: Is the air surrounding you masculine or feminine? Why? Might it change from one to the other sometimes? Is the light masculine or feminine? The wind? That banana slug? How much can you notice around you — color, smells, feelings, temperature, texture — to which you can apply these words? How do these words feel in your body when you apply them to elements in your surroundings? What happens when you apply these two words to yourself? What feels right? What feels limited? What doesn't fit?

There are no right answers to any of these questions. This is not a trick exercise. Some people find that it diminishes the distinction between the concepts of masculine and feminine. Others find that they can distinguish quite strongly between the two. For some, it's a little of both. Some people don't resonate with this process at all. Whatever happens in your case, every response you have to this activity will tell you something about yourself.

Before you leave the place in which you've been reflecting, thank your surroundings for helping you. And when you get home, pull out your journal. Writing down the results of this reflection will make it much more powerful, allowing you to participate in a process that utilizes both hand and head, feeling and thinking.

Gaia

She has been at my left side now for fifteen years. That is, I have seen her there for that long; I know that she has been there all of my life. More than once, she has saved my life. Often she sits beside me when I meditate, her huge head resting on equally huge paws. I've seen her running ahead of me on the steep trail up Teton Canyon. One bleak afternoon in a cramped oncologist's office a long time ago, I watched her lift her leg on an intern's pants leg and let loose with a blast of yellow urine.

Her name is Gaia, and it suites her. She is a gray wolf, larger than any I have ever seen, colored silver and black. Her toenails are like small ebony river stones, and her eyes are yellow and dauntingly intelligent. Above my desk hangs

a drawing of her, and on my meditation table is a small bronze statue in her likeness, howling. She walks across certain territories of my life, showing herself to me in dreamtime, in visualizations, and in that misty landscape that stretches between wakefulness and sleep. The only place I do not see her regularly is in "the square world" — the term I use for ordinary, physical reality. And yet there have been times, one time in particular, when she has pierced the filmy netting between this world and all the many others, and has peeked out at me for a brief and startling instant.

I met Gaia formally in a program that taught active visualization to cancer patients. It is believed that the most effective images to combat cancer are those that resonate emotionally with the patient. In our group of about twenty-five, we conjured up a family of wasps, a football team, a sumo wrestler, two knights in jousting gear, an angel, a SWAT team, and a lot of animals. I found Gaia. Another woman called in a wolf with a different name. From that day forward, I began a conscious relationship with what in ancient shamanic terms would be called a power animal, although I knew nothing of such traditions at that time.

For many months, I met dutifully with Gaia three times a day in a formal meditation/visualization practice. My lymphatic system reacted to my inner visions by boosting my cancer-fighting cells 20 percent in six weeks. Gaia was at work saving my life, cell by cell. One day, of her own volition, she stepped out of the cramped confines of my daily practice and started appearing to me at other times as well. The first time she surfaced this new way, I was shopping downtown when suddenly I sensed her off to my left. I can't say why walking down the sidewalk with an imaginary wolf at my side caused me to walk taller and puff out my chest, but it did, and it felt marvelous.

In many indigenous traditions, it is not wise to speak of your power animal, or to mention its name, ever. But I speak to you of Gaia because now it is important to speak of these things, and to bring these indigenous gifts back to life. It is urgent that we remember this piece, this gift, of our humanness. Gaia agrees. The world of spirit power is uncharted territory so far as our culture is concerned, and Gaia is most at home in uncharted territory. Furthermore, she has never indicated to me, in her way, that I should keep her under wraps.

Gaia is as real to me as the dogs in my family, as the air, as this maple desk I write from. Many people might see this proclamation as crazy, or at least "out there," but I know that even today, belief in the reality of animal spirits is more common in human experience around the world than not. In a time not so very far past, and for tens of thousands of years before that, this belief was a universal knowing among all people in all lands, and so I feel that I am in good and sane company.

While all wolves in the world are not Gaia, I believe that all the living wolves and dog-wolves who have crossed my path were visitations or emissaries on behalf of Gaia. Some of the wolves I have known have come to me in books or movies, and all have evoked a piece of the mystery that I feel in Gaia's presence. I would liken this to saying that in a puzzle, all the pieces carry a message or an aspect of the whole, completed. Gaia is the whole of my Wolf puzzle, and her emissaries the odd-shaped pieces.

Throughout my life, all of my wolf encounters have had one thing in common: I have felt an electrical charge of fascination or "recognition" at the sight of each one, and the energetic hit would stay with me for hours, sometimes days or years. My very first meeting with a Gaia emissary was nebulous but characteristically intense and magnetic. In a rare moment of early childhood television watching, I stumbled across a very old movie with a dog hero in it. My mother never let us turn on the TV set during the day unless we were sick, and "sick" meant we had to have a temperature or be vomiting, so I'm sure I was quite ill. I could not have been more than five years old. The movie looked as close to a silent film as they get, and the characters were all speaking in scratchy, brittle tones that bespoke old, old celluloid.

The story was about a group of young children who found a German shepherd in the woods and named him Wolf. I could not yet readily distinguish between this Wolf and real wolves. He certainly looked wolfy enough to me. Wolf saved the children's lives daily. He was huge compared to them, with tall ears and a dark, serious face. The children hid him away in the trunk of a burned-out tree so that no one would know about him. At the end of the movie, a military figure showed up looking for him and blew a silent dog whistle. Wolf — evidently an AWOL soldier — was compelled to respond and came leaping out of the tree stump, running at full tilt toward the soldier. All the children were bawling and saying, "No, Wolf! Go back! Please go baaack!!" At this point I was bawling loudly along with them. For weeks afterward, I imagined that Wolf was mine, and that I had him hidden away under my bed.

My next wolf visitor was similar to the first. Also named Wolf, he too came along masquerading in German shepherd form, and again in a movie, where he was the protector of an orphaned girl. I imagined my way into the life of this orphan and would gladly have traded away my parents and home for the chance to be befriended by Wolf.

When I was eight years old, my family welcomed our

very first dog. She was a German shepherd, a breed that at that point in my life was indistinguishable from wolves. Our new dog was black and silver and beautiful. Of course, I campaigned hard to name her Wolf, but because she was a she, no one would go along with me on this. We agreed on "Lady." Her life with us was tragically brief, and soon another German shepherd joined our family — coal black, fierce, and protective, with the misleading name of Sugar. At first, Sugar would come to no one but me and would stand guard at the entrance of my bedroom door all night, even warding off my parents with a low growl. She walked beside me like a shadow wherever I went, and I secretly called her Wolf. She was the Wolf of my dreams, and for a few glorious weeks, I imagined myself the orphan girl with my wolf-dog protector. When she turned her attention to other members of the family and settled in as guardian of us all, I felt abandoned and lost and reconciled myself to calling her Sugar.

By this time in my life — the beginnings of my double-digit years — I was an insatiable reader, and my favorite books were populated by wolf and wolf-dog characters: The Silver Chief series, Jack London's books, and books about the lives and habits of wild wolves. One book told the true story of a family who raised a wolf from a cub. They kept the wolf's identity a secret and told neighbors she was an Alaskan malamute mix.

The year Sugar died, I was eighteen and about to leave home for my first summer job in the Teton Mountains. Her sudden death from pneumonia marked the passing of an era and heralded the close of my childhood. One thing that didn't change, though, was my affinity for and enchantment with wolves. Gaia's call whispered on into my young adult years.

Had I been born in another, earlier time, I would have known that Wolf, whom I later called Gaia, was my power animal, the one who had chosen to walk beside me through life. My parents would have encouraged this knowing in me, and honored it. But I was a child of twentieth-century America, where enchantment with a particular animal is known only as a hobby or a childhood phase to be outgrown. Here we humor children and indulge them for their magical, mysterious relationships. We have forgotten as a people to honor such things.

The summer after Sugar died, I searched for a puppy for myself — a very specific puppy. I wanted a shepherd-malamute mix, and I found her in a six-week ball of fuzz named Keesha. Please do not ask me why I didn't name her Wolf. To this day, I wonder about that myself. For the next ten-and-a-half years, Keesha was the four-footed version of my soul. We were inseparable. The best of what I imagined I could ever be, I projected onto Keesha, and she rose to the challenge. Brilliant, beautiful, intuitive, and charismatic, Keesha turned heads wherever we went. Many people asked me if she was part coyote or wolf. Sometimes, I said yes. I walked very tall and strong and proud for all the years she walked at my side.

Keesha was the carrier of my soul, and her guardianship of me took a shocking, traumatic, and I believe destined turn when she developed an ugly and malignant tumor in her mouth, the same place my own cancerous tumor would show up years later. Keesha lived only a few scant weeks after her diagnosis, and her death ripped me to shreds. When she died I lost a part of myself that I have been reconstructing ever since; in charging her to carry my soul, I had made no efforts to carry it myself, and that core work continues in me to this day.

Shortly after Keesha's passing, a call came into the humane society where I worked as an educator. "There is a wolf loose on the golf course! Can you please send an officer?" Officer Griggs was quickly dispatched, and we all chuckled to ourselves as he drove off. The "wolf" would be a big malamute or husky stray, just like the "rattlesnakes" we were called to remove always turned out to be harmless gopher snakes.

I was passing by the front desk when Officer Griggs came in, a shell-shocked look on his face. On the end of a broken chain was an animal that was clearly no dog: Yellow eyes, shoulders as high as my hips, shaggy silver coat, and feet bigger than my splayed hands — this was unmistakably a wolf. I saw no shred of dog in his eyes, in his face, in his body. A rush of wild wind gusted in the door on his heels and blew us all into stunned silence. He sat himself down regally on bony haunches and looked at us, flashing a heady grin. He'd had a good, long romp on the golf course and was obviously quite pleased with himself. As his mouth sagged open and his tongue rolled out like a coil of pink flypaper, his enormous canines announced his lineage and his age: He was only a pup, probably no more than eight months old.

For three weeks the wolf lived at the shelter, mostly in my care. In his way, he touched the weeping wound in my heart that Keesha had left behind and licked my soul into the first stages of healing. I discovered that he had an owner nearby, a young bearded man who had rescued him from a filthy kennel when he was only eight weeks old and who could no longer keep him. "You should see my house," he groaned. "He's made a den in the sofa, ripped the plaster off the walls, eaten through doors, and peed everywhere. Can you help him?"

The man had called the pup Steppenwolf, after the Hermann Hesse novel, but I renamed him Wolff and took him on as my special project, eventually finding him a permanent placement at a wildlife rescue facility that was starting up a new wolf pack. I adored Wolff — the feel of his impossibly dense fur, the earthy smell of him, the weight of his huge paw grabbing at my arm. He taught me that wolves and dogs have been apart for a long, long time. His strength, his intelligence, his sheer presence were at a level of magnificence to which no dog could aspire. And yet he had his doggy ways, too — the way he would romp with me, the attitude of his plumed tail so much like Keesha's, and the dog-like trust in his smile. Through Wolff, I noticed the wolf-ways of the kennel strays and unwanted dogs — the hint of his dignity in their eyes and tails and faces. The day he left — as he had come, on the end of a long chain — he looked back at me before he climbed confidently into the truck, and flashed me that smile. For an instant, his eyes held me. They hold me still. It was not too long after he left the shelter that I left it, too.

For the next few years I remained blessedly unaware that Keesha's passing had foreshadowed my own coming journey with catastrophic illness. And when the cancer found me, Keesha was no longer there to carry me through it. Yet in profound ways, she *was* there, and she *did* carry me. I know that Keesha was a puzzle piece of Gaia in her mysterious spiritual infancy, a psychopomp — along with Lady and Sugar — between dog and wolf, a domestic version of an energy and power I now needed in its most wild state. And Wolff had carried me to the next level of my journey — to the fully potent Wolf spirit. All the many puzzle pieces of Gaia, in all her forms and genders, had readied me for my encounter with her.

Midway through radiation treatments for metastatic head-and-neck cancer, I met Gaia at the end of a long day of guided dancing and drawing, near the close of my nine-week cancer visualization program. She simply walked across my inner field of vision, looked at me, and sat down and waited. She looked exactly like Wolff, but with a slightly more feminine cast to her face. In her right ear she carried a disk-shaped talisman with several raven feathers dangling from it. "It can't be a wolf," I argued in my head. "It is too obvious. I must have forced myself to imagine this. I'm not worthy.... Susan, who do you think you are to walk with *this* animal?"

I pushed the wolf aside and went back to the computer Pacman image I had been working with. It had been so easy, and so deadly, to fall into this imagery — sterile, nonliving, small, and yellow, a head without a body, nothing but a mouth opening and closing. Cancer had flattened me in those early days, and it left me feeling frail and ashamed. Yes, that's the correct word. Ashamed. I don't know of a cancer patient who at one time or another hasn't feared that the curse has come to them because they deserved it in some way, who hasn't struggled with feelings of shame and unworthiness. Although I would never have said it out loud and could not even say it to myself, I believed then that I had been proclaimed unworthy for life, and so life was being taken from me.

Refusing to be butted out by the yellow computer mouthman, the wolf strutted back onto my mental screen and gave me her name: Gaia. There remained some small part of me that cancer had not obliterated. She spoke to that part, and it heard her call. In that moment, I began working with her image for my survival.

My diagnosis was a horrid one, and I was told that I would most likely be dead within two years. Fear was all I saw registered in the eyes around me, and in every mirror I looked into. The "real world" had become a terrifying, lonely place that stopped feeling real the day my doctor told me he was "so very sorry...." Gaia's world was a safe house, peaceful, sustaining, nonjudgmental. The times I spent there in my mind visiting her were the times I felt the strongest, the most confident and hopeful. Who is to say that the world we visited together was only in my imagination?

"Imagination," says long-time shamanic practitioner and teacher Amy Cortese, "was not a word in the old languages. Journeys were real, no matter if they were taken in our minds, or dreams, or on a dirt path." Shamanism is the most ancient spiritual system known in human record. One of its most defining and controversial features is the self-induced visionary experience that connects the practitioner to spirit beings who guide, guard, heal, instruct, or bless. Many of these spirit beings are animals.

I believe now that in my modern and unknowing way, I had somehow tapped into that ancestral shamanic world with Gaia. It is not hard to do. In fact, I feel that we are biologically hard-wired through evolution for relationships with animal and nature spirits. This tradition has lived in humankind, in our very bones, for far longer than any of our Western spiritual traditions. Practices that have survived for tens of thousands of years have done so because they support life and living. They work. The recent global upswell in shamanic studies and indigenous spirituality speaks to our soul-longing and affinity for these uniquely human rites and customs.

In the traditions of shamanism, one is advised to honor the animal spirits that come to offer assistance, and I felt naturally compelled to do that for Gaia. I began filling my house with images of wolves, from posters and paintings to calendars and statues. Around my neck I wore a silver necklace of a wolf paw print. I bought tapes of wolves singing, and I visited captive wolves in rescue facilities like Wolf Haven in Washington state. The months passed, and my cancer did not return. To the surprise and disbelief of every doctor I have seen since, it has never returned.

When I began working on my first book, *Animals as Teachers and Healers,* I wrote about Gaia, and about wolves, and about healing. All of life conspires with us in spirit: It was during the writing of that book and its special tribute to wolves that wild wolves were being reintroduced to Yellowstone National Park, and that same year I made the decision to move up to that area of the Rockies. It was not the lure of the wolves that persuaded me to make that move — at least, I don't think it was — but the idea that I might someday see a wolf living in the wild, or hear it howl nearby, was exciting.

Curiously, the one landscape where I had never met Gaia in any of her guises was in her true, wild home.

The winter after I moved to the Tetons, a wolf pack from Yellowstone came to live on the National Elk Refuge, just a few miles from my house. I fully expected I would see some members of the pack. I had lived with wolves in my internal healing landscape for so long, and of course I assumed Gaia would take this special opportunity to appear to me in the flesh. I searched for her — or at least for her relatives — with binoculars and sighting scopes for that entire winter. Spring came and the pack left, making no effort to find me, as far as I could tell. What's more, not one other person I knew who had looked for the wolves had been disappointed. Just me. I took it personally, and then felt ashamed for my naive assumptions. Gaia clearly had her own agenda, and showing me her spirit in the living wild was not on it, at least not then.

On a cold, windy September morning several years later, I walked along the banks of the Snake River with my two dogs, Arrow and Strongheart. From the riverbank, I could see the outline of my tiny, old rental cabin through the cottonwoods. Sadness blew like bitter wind through my heart; the landlord wanted the cabin back. I could simply not imagine living anywhere else. It was home to me, like one's skin is home. Packing the boxes to move was an agony, so I ran off often with the dogs to walk this place that was as cherished to me as my soul, this place that soon I would walk only as a trespasser on private property.

Strongheart was on a leash that morning, and Arrow trotted a few feet ahead. Suddenly, Arrow burst out with a series of high-pitched barks. She bounded forward, then

paused and whirled back to stand in front of me, her tail up
like a flag. Strongheart lurched forward and jerked me ahead
a few feet until I dropped the lead. The dogs were giving me
every indicator that a coyote was up ahead in the willows. A
crow called out close by.

About twenty yards ahead, a dog-like figure drifted out
from the willows, paused to face us, and then moved silently
as smoke, down the dry riverbed into the aspens.

Strongheart froze. Arrow silenced in mid-yip. It was over
so fast that only the memory of the creature remained, im-
printed like a misty transparency over the landscape: silver
and black, with yellow eyes that glinted back at us even at
that distance. I measured my memory of the animal's size
against the tall, broken stems of moose-eaten willow that had
served as a backdrop. It was no coyote. I walked hesitantly
up the cobbled riverbed to where the phantom had crossed.
There were no tracks, no shiver of motion in the bushes.
Nothing. The dogs remained silent and poised, the hair full
up on their backs, but they displayed no interest in tracking
the elusive creature. Nor did I. It was clear who we had seen.
Sitting down on the stones, I wept.

Picking up a small gray pebble from the riverbed, I whispered a thank-you to whatever hand it was that had held
aside the veil for one precious instant and allowed me a humbling glimpse into that other landscape, that very real place
that I do not call imagination.

Mysterious Relations

THE TRUTH ABOUT FANTASY

When I examine myself and my methods of thought,
I come to the conclusion that the gift of fantasy has meant
more to me than my talent for absorbing positive knowledge.

— Albert Einstein

"I write fantasy. You know, words are so limiting sometimes. It seems to me that the best way to describe what I want to say is by putting just enough fantasy into my nonfiction so that people wonder if it is 'real' or not."

In a funky café in Boulder, Colorado, I am visiting with a radio host who sports a mane of the most curly golden hair I've ever seen. As she talks about her writing, she holds a mug of cappuccino in one hand and sets up a trunk of ancient equipment on a tabletop with the other. Settling in for a live radio interview, I am utterly smitten with Boulder. It seems a place where everyone does yoga, has visions, and says profound things all the time. I imagine that if I lived here, I, too, might say profound things all the time, and for a fleeting instant, I think I will move here. Yup — right now.

I had been ruminating for days about my own book, *Heart in the Wild,* perplexed at the propensity of certain readers to take literally some of the passages I was using to illuminate an idea, a perspective that was not linear, not easy to get my hands around. I had used vision and fantasy, but never with the intention of misleading anyone. On the contrary, my intent had been to make true and absorbable ideas that were simply beyond our cultural ken. But people were coming up to me in bookshops saying, "So an elk really spoke to you! You heard it! Wow! It came into your bedroom!!"

Yes... and no. Yes, Elk came to me. He came to me over and over, sometimes in physical reality, and often in sleeping dreams and waking visions. He came to me as Gaia had come over the years. No, a bull elk in the flesh never came into my bedroom and plopped down next to me. His antlers would never have fit through the door. Was I lying, then? I certainly didn't think so. Still, I was finding myself in the odd position of having to say to groups of people, "Yes, the elk in my pasture were really there. No, the elk in my room wasn't. No, he didn't speak to me in English. Yes, he did speak to me. Yes, the antler he left for me is real...."

A scant twenty minutes later, my radio interview was over. I set my elbows on the fish-mosaic tabletop and leaned in close to the radio host and said, "What is fantasy anyhow? And what is real?" She fixed me with a quick, conspiratorial grin as she grabbed up her purse and microphones and hurried out into the Boulder sunshine, calling back to me over her shoulder, "It's all real — don't you think?" I wondered if somehow she knew about my antelope.

You see, I have this antelope. Actually, I have his head. It is mounted and hangs on a log support post that holds up my living room ceiling. It was a gift from a contractor, who had three other antelope heads hanging on his walls, all of which had larger horns than the mount he gave to me. Perhaps because his horns were not so impressive as the others, my gift antelope was no longer worthy of the contractor's wall and had been stuffed into a recycled gym locker.

Animal heads on walls give me the chills. Seeing one stuffed into a storage locker seemed even creepier, if that's possible. The contractor saw me staring at the head with my mouth hanging open and — misjudging my look as one of profound desire — asked me if I wanted it. So I said yes — anything to get it off the pile of old rags and extension cords. In a slight daze, I placed the antelope head in the back of my car, his nose pointed resolutely toward the sky, and drove home. For a long time, the antelope sat on the floor of my bedroom, contemplating the ceiling with his huge glass eyes. He had a delicate face, slender snout, and the most lovely and expressive mouth you can imagine. I looked up the spirit meaning of Antelope and found that these creatures hold the energy for direct and firm action, taken *now*. That seemed good energy to have in one's life, so I mounted him finally — and self-consciously — over my bed.

Before hanging him up, I smudged my antelope with cedar smoke and sage, sent him words of honor and respect, and asked that his spirit know that he was seen and appreciated — and mourned. How I longed to see him in his full body, alive and running, with eyes that could blink away the dust of the Wyoming prairie. I draped a beautiful medicine bag and a beaded necklace around him and tied a blue heron feather to his ear. Each night before sleep, I thanked him for watching over me.

Now, several moves later, he holds court over my living

room. Many people who come to my cabin for the first time look at him, and then at me, quizzically. I can see the question: "Self-professed animal lover hangs dead animals in her house?" All I can say is what is true for me: This creature ended up in my hands by a strange turn of events, and I am trying to honor him as best I can and learn what the meaning of his gift is. I don't have all this figured out yet, not by a long shot. I know only that I could not leave him stuffed in a metal locker.

Since moving him into the living room, I have noticed something quite remarkable about this antelope. He has taken to coming down off the post at night, slipping into his sleek, shimmering body, and tiptoeing all around the house. I hear the soft padding of his cloven feet on the thick carpet downstairs, and sometimes I see him peering around the corner to the kitchen when I come down for a late-night cookie and mug of tea. The dogs lift their heads to watch him, cocking their ears to the side.

All night long, he roams the open plains of my downstairs, sniffing the old wheat-colored shag carpet, traipsing around the boulders of furniture, nibbling on the Boston fern, resting beneath the huge old jade tree near the propane stove. He seems happy enough. Sometimes, when I glance at him sideways, he nods at me from his place on the wall and firelight shimmers off his ebony horns, sprouting like twin saplings just above his eye sockets.

I've told several of my friends about his nighttime meanderings, and they smile and nod. They know that there are many things more real in life than what we can touch. Most of them have spirits who flit on paws or fairy wings through the doorways of their own homes. The elemental spirits that visit Teresa's house left her a collection of tiny crystal grains in a spiral bowl she keeps. Two buffalo spirits battled through the night with snorts and thumps when David put their skulls next to each other on his kitchen table. At his neighbor's house, a bear skull made everyone sick until it was placed in a location of honor and offered prayers.

We all know beyond any doubt that as humans, we cannot see all the color spectrums that exist, nor hear beyond a certain frequency of sound. We are limited to certain dimensions of reality, and science and physics remind us that much of what we know to be true is beyond our human capacity to experience. If we acknowledge that there is much of our own, known reality that eludes us, might there then be worlds of consciousness, other dimensions, and other realities that exist completely — or perhaps nearly completely — outside our awareness?

What do we gain by making our world so small that it excludes the wonder of all these fascinating possibilities? My antelope nods to this, and he has some questions of his own. He wonders why so many of us human animals give over to culture and to others our own power to decide what is real and what isn't. And then he asks me if I know what is real? I answer "It's all real, don't you think?" And we both listen to Gaia howl from the bedroom.

A Practice

What if someone suddenly granted you the power to decide what is true and what is not? What is real and what is not?

What is imagination and what is not? I'm granting that to you now. Poof! There — it's done.

Are there places, things, or creatures in your home that have always held special significance for you? A picture, an animal companion, a statue, a plant, a childhood toy? A corner of your garden? Shrug off all your preconceived notions about this thing or this place, along with the cultural tales and constraints surrounding your beliefs. Is there another meaning that emerges when you hold up the bowl of unlimited possibilities?

Do you have a rose bush that speaks to you, a tree who stands guard over your home, a statue of an angel or a frog that stretches to life when you sleep and visits you in your dreams? Is your dog truly your best friend? Your cat a Buddha? What if you added all these things to your "What's Real and True" list? Whose is the voice that tells you that you can't? And who does that voice serve? Is it a voice of love and possibility and healing?

Is the voice yours? Come, have a talk with my antelope about that.

Strongheart

Strongheart has appeared often enough in my writing, but I have never told his full story outside of my circle of friends, and never on paper. Writing always brings me to the deeper meaning of things and reveals new insights to me as the words spill onto the computer screen and develop a life of their own. Sometimes writing reveals things I didn't know, or wish I didn't have to know. If you write, you know this. If you begin writing, you will discover this.

I'll just say this straight out and go on from here. Strongheart is the most magnificent, beautiful, mushy, huge, and expressive dog to ever grace my life. And he is a lethal animal. Because of a series of circumstances, some of which I will explore with you here, I am keeper of a dog who has

the potential to kill. If you wrote me your own story of a Strongheart-style dog and asked me for advice, I would tell you, as kindly as I could, never to keep such a dog, and never to pass the dog along to another keeper. It is a simple, straightforward bit of advice, offered in a seriousness that allows no room for fudging.

More than any animal who has ever come into my life, Strongheart is the bearer of lessons, paradoxes, dreams, and fears. He is my most in-your-face catalyst for constant, daily re-evaluation of my beliefs, convictions, and spiritual path.

This is his story. I will frame it in the context of safety and fear, empowerment and projection. I could tell it a thousand other ways as well. Perhaps over the years, I will.

Six years ago, I lived surrounded by a sea of animals. Our property in Oregon, the home I called Brightstar Farm, consisted of just one small acre. And so I populated it with small creatures: mini-donkeys, mini-sheep, a mini-llama, and banty chickens. I walked among them all like Gulliver among the Lilliputians. Because every animal that graced our farm was diminutive, Brightstar quickly became a prime watering hole for coyotes, pumas, and — mostly — neighborhood dogs looking for a buffet. It was as though I had hung out a neon "Eat Here" sign. Arrow, my collie-shepherd cross, had it in her mind that the only creature our farm family needed protection from was a large squirrel who lived in a pine tree near the house, and her attention was fully focused on him and him alone. She welcomed other predators into our yard with much fanfare and tail wagging. I think she believed they had come to help her keep the evil squirrel treed.

On the afternoon I returned from work to find my neighbor's yellow Labs in my fenced yard for the third time, running my very pregnant miniature donkeys to exhaustion, I marched over to my computer and looked up "livestock guarding dogs" on the Internet. Four months later, I flew down to San Diego and brought Strongheart home. A purebred Anatolian Shepherd Dog puppy, his ancestors hailed from Turkey, where these massive dogs have protected sheep flocks for thousands of years. I named him after Jay Allen Boone's beloved German shepherd companion in his classic book, *Kinship with All Life*. At that time, I had no idea how completely he would live up to his name.

At barely five months of age, Strongheart was eighty-six pounds of puppy, all white and all legs, ears, and feet — feet of a size you can only imagine. I chose his particular breed for several reasons: They are long-lived for a giant breed, they do not drool, and — I confess this with embarrassment — all the write-ups on the Internet were captivating. Strongheart and his sisters and parents were actually the first live Anatolians I had ever even seen.

I believed myself to be a woman who knew dogs, and so I had no concerns or hesitations when I went down to fetch Strongheart — my first male dog — carrying the largest crate the airlines would allow. I was blissfully nonplused when I saw his sire, all one-hundred-forty pounds of him, with jaws as massive as a bear trap. I had not a care in the world when the breeder asked me if I had any experience with livestock guarding dogs and handed me a stack of reading material. No concerns, even, when every puppy in the litter gamboled up to me for pets and rubs except Strongheart, who rested quietly on a hill above me and showed no interest in getting cozy at all. Only years later would I remember that day and realize that I had missed clear signals that Strongheart was the alpha puppy in his group.

His first night with us was blessedly uneventful. The airline trip had been a horror for him, and when I opened his crate at the airport, he had vomited and messed on himself in fear. He rode home in our truck with his smelly head in my lap, looking up at me with the most soulful, adoring brown eyes I have ever seen on a dog. When he placed his huge paw on my heart as we drove, raking me with his white claws, I fell in love with him, instantly and fiercely.

On Day Two, when I let both dogs into the back yard, Strongheart assumed a position on the porch with his front paws crossed and his long white back pressed up against the sliding patio door. Arrow never came near the back door all day. When I called her to me, I saw her look warily at Strongheart and ignore me. Strongheart had his eyes on her, and she would not venture forward under that gaze. Nor would Mirella, the cat. Thinking this was all just the jockeying dynamics of a new creature in the family, I dismissed it.

On Day Three, our best friends came to visit when we were not home. They called me later that evening to tell me that Strongheart had looked at them so "oddly" that they did not feel it would be okay to come into the yard and say hello to our new family member, our "puppy." We all thought this quite amusing and cute. "He thinks he's king!" we joked to ourselves. To Strongheart, of course, this was no joke. He was fulfilling the call of thousands of years of selective breeding that guided him to protect and to lead. Making his own judgments about what and who needed protection was his birthright, his calling. Given his development, breeding, and gender, he assumed he was the leader unless someone else stepped forward. All dogs — and all people, actually — exhibit their genetic makeup to some degree or another. I simply did not know that I had selected a dog who would take his calling to such a serious level.

On Day Four I ran out of the house at the sound of a dog fight in my back yard. Arrow was standing on the lawn, confused and bleeding. Strongheart stood at the back door, hackles up like a white wave, tail vibrating, fangs displayed. His eyes were fixed on Arrow. They were not the soft eyes he had shown in the truck only a few days back. Someone else was home in there. Someone I didn't know at all. He did not look like a puppy anymore. When I shouted his name and said, "Leave it!" he turned to me with his eyes melting swiftly to soft and adoring pools and hung his head. Shaking, I called Arrow and he let her pass into the house, where I wiped the blood off her bitten ear. Although not a serious bite, it was an omen I did not dismiss.

The next week I called Strongheart's breeder, logged onto livestock guardian dog e-mail lists, and read everything I could find about Anatolians. Armed with new and helpful knowledge — which I should have had before I ever brought Strongheart home — I decided that I was woman enough for the job of leader in our family, and that I could learn how to convey this idea to Strongheart. I also made an appointment with my veterinarian to neuter Strongheart by the end of the week.

I have lived all my life with highly domesticated dogs, creatures whose life joy is to please their people and who accept leadership easily and without question. In all my years in humane work, going in and out of kennels each day and handling thousands of dogs, I had fooled myself into thinking that I knew dogs. We are enculturated to think of dogs as safe, plush toys that move. But Strongheart was not going to let me live with such foolishness. In his way he would teach me — among many other things — a new respect for the presence, autonomy, and wild nature of dogs.

Over the next two years, Strongheart regularly tested me

by getting rough with Arrow, lying in doorways and refusing to move, getting growly when I tried to cut his toenails, developing selective hearing around the words "come" and "no," and even deciding he needed to sleep on my bed. To this day, he will take these maneuvers out and parade them around until I take charge again. And then he relaxes into a mush-puddle, all sighs, calf-eyes, and wiggle-tail, happy to know that he does not have to be master and that he can relinquish that heavy and dangerous responsibility to me.

Mostly, I reaffirm my leader status in very undramatic ways. I don't let him in or out of doors before me. I make him sit for his food or any other treat. I make sure that I can always take food and bones and anything else out of his mouth. If he growls at me, I pretty much ignore him and do what I need to do, and then make him go away and lie on his bed for awhile. He knows exactly what these time-outs are all about.

I am going to keep the good news going here a bit longer before I carry us down a more difficult path. From the day I brought Strongheart home, no animal in our care has ever been molested by anyone or anything. His Anatolian stare-down has been enough to keep predators of any type out of our yard. Strongheart has rarely had to do battle to get his point across, and he has never seriously harmed another animal. His presence and his confidence are enough. Except for me, I do not believe there is anything or anyone he ranks higher than himself. I have never seen such confidence in a dog, and I have seen it only rarely in people. It is not bully energy I am talking about. It is sheer, undiluted assuredness in self and calling.

I am a woman who has lived my life afraid of many things. I have harbored a sense of fear in living alone in cities and towns. Especially at night, I worry about open windows, about coming home late and getting safely to the front door, about making a mistake in an isolated parking lot and finding myself in sudden and terrifying danger. I have not felt utterly safe walking woodland trails or camping, and my fear is not so much about nature, but about the twisted and dark nature of some members of my own species. I have been afraid, also, of what I call the Boogeyman, a primal object of fear with no face. It creeps up on me in adulthood as it did in childhood, when I decided it lived under my bed.

There is a stark difference in my mind between caution and fear, and I am admitting to you that I have not been merely cautious, but fearful. Strongheart changed that. In the years he has been with me, I have released any fear I have harbored about assault or violence against me, including — or especially — my fear of the Boogeyman. Fear trickled away so quietly I hardly realized it was gone until I noticed that I was relishing my open windows on summer nights, that I was no longer hesitating even a fraction of a second before putting my key in the door and walking into my dark, empty house. I take long, luxurious night walks into the moonlit mountains with Strongheart, my lifelong fear of the dark transformed into a profound and intoxicating enchantment with it. Beyond time, space, or physical reality, Strongheart keeps me safe, as he keeps whatever he claims as his own.

It was when he was around two years of age that Strongheart began having "incidents." These involved strange men who came onto the property unannounced, like delivery or repair folks who chose to ignore our clearly posted "Keep Out!" and "Beware of the Dog" signs. Strongheart tore more than one shirt and ripped the back pants pockets off those who would not stop and stand still when he told them to. Now, keep in mind that I live in rural country where everyone has a farm dog, and most all of these dogs snarl and bark and go nuts when you come onto their property. As a general rule, visitors ignore the show and just head for the door. But that isn't something you can do at our house. Pushing past Strongheart is not acceptable to him. It is a most dire threat to his family. All of the ancestors who live in his cells tell him this, and he tried to tell me this himself by tearing clothes and roaring.

Has there ever been a tiny voice on your shoulder that you've managed to completely ignore until it is too late? Then you say, "Those signs have been there for months"? For a long time, luck protected our 'intruders,' and Strongheart didn't hurt anyone. But then one awful day, luck stopped saving Strongheart and me.

My mother and I had just returned to the Teton Mountains, where we were going to look for a place to buy and settle and live. And I mean "just returned." We were in our rental house for not twenty minutes when I heard the explosive roar by the front door. Now Strongheart always travels poorly. I'd had to put him on tranquilizers for two days, and he was probably as confused and tired as we were. I had fastened him on a cable out front, which was about the worst thing I could have possibly done to him: He was secured to a new home and strange surroundings, and not completely in his right mind. Unfortunately, I was not the one who would suffer the consequences. Ben did — Ben, the former tenant who came back to get something, to tell me something.

I heard Ben's voice calling me from out front just as I heard Strongheart's roar. I yelled from the bedroom, "Strongheart! Leave it! Ben...wait!" and I raced to the door with my stomach vaulting into my throat. When I got to the door, Ben was holding Strongheart's head in his hands, and Strongheart was quiet. His eyes were locked on Ben's face, and his body was stiff. Ben thought all was well. But I knew the stare and the silence that followed his roaring were the last stage before an attack. Strongheart lunged at Ben the moment I touched the screen door handle. And I saw it all in slow motion as I see it replayed in my mind over and over, still: Strongheart roaring and ripping Ben's shirt sleeve, Ben pulling to the side, yelling "Whoa...whoa...whoa!" Strongheart ducking behind Ben and reaching for the pant leg, all the while bellowing in a sound that was like no dog, but an enraged lion.

Strongheart grabbed and released Ben's upper leg, then came running to me with his head hanging and his tail low. Ben was still on his feet, reeling. We were all in shock. Strongheart sank to the ground and curled up in ball. His teeth were clacking spasmodically, and he was drooling. I ran over to Ben and we stared at each other wide-eyed. Ben's shirt was nearly ripped off. There were four perfect holes in his jeans, and he would not let me have a look at the damage. "Ben, please, please, let me see..."

"It's okay, I'm alright, it'll be okay," he kept saying over and over, and I knew he was speaking from some place other than his right senses. As if on automatic pilot, he told me what he had come to tell me, and he walked to the shed to get what he had left behind. Then he drove away, assuring me that all was just fine. I knew it was not fine. Numbness and freezing cold overtook my entire body. I quickly brought Strongheart into the house and shut the door. When I began mindlessly unpacking my car, my hands were shaking and my heart was racing at a terrible gallop.

Strongheart snuck away to his special bed, the first item I unpacked, and stayed there, scarcely leaving it for two days. His ears stayed low, and his eyes took on that lost and far-away look that tells me he is depressed. He ate little and sighed much throughout the days, his broad sides heaving up and down like a bellows. Was he distressed from the attack, or was he responding to my own misery and upset from the event? I imagined both.

Two days after the attack, a friend called, prefacing her words with "I just feel that is it my responsibility to tell you this..." Ben had visited her and told her the story of what had happened with an openness he had not had the strength to share with me. My friend said that Ben believed that Strongheart had tried to kill him. His leg was purple and black from hip to knee, and the medical people at the clinic told him that the bite wounds were an inch and a half deep. Blessedly, there was no arterial or nerve damage. Strongheart did not grab and shake like a shark or a coyote might have, but simply the size of his teeth made them lethal. I shuddered to think what could have happened if those teeth had hit a main artery. Or a throat.

When I called Ben to talk more deeply and to pay for his

medical bill, he said the same to me in a nearly apologetic voice: "Susan, I think he wanted to kill me." I told Ben that I was at a terrible and fearful crossroads with my dog. And Ben said that he was glad he had been the "test case" for this serious bite. "He was defending his property, and I just didn't listen to him. He had a right to do what he did." Ben filed no charges.

But that was not the end of it, and I cannot vouch for the right of a dog to bite a person. For weeks afterward, I sat at my altar in the evening, trying to come to terms with what had happened through silence, concentration, and prayer. Sometimes Strongheart sat with me, resting his head on my lap like a warm white melon. I wrote the e-mail lists of owners of Anatolians, sharing my story and asking for advice. Is he an anomaly? Is he vicious? Do these dogs do this? Did my dog try to kill this man? What do I do?

The answers were compassionate, consistent, and direct: "Strongheart was not trying to kill Ben. If he had meant to do that, it would have happened silently and so swiftly you could scarcely have seen it." "Do not ever cable one of these dogs. There is no worse thing you could have done." "Yes, some of these dogs do this. They are the ones who are dispatched swiftly in their home country if they show aggression to the community." Many reminded me that if Strongheart had been the size of a beagle, the event would not have seemed so terrifying. "For Strongheart, this was a swift nip. It's the size of his teeth that put it all into a different ballgame."

These are the things I asked and still ask myself: Is it ethical to keep a dog who can kill someone — even if that is not his intention? Should I have his teeth pulled or filed? What was I thinking, remaining so oblivious to Strongheart's warnings for so many years? How stupid can a person be? Is there any way to keep him 100 percent safe in my care? Should I have him humanely destroyed before I make another mistake? But mostly I asked, Why is this dog with me? Why?

Many people who have met Strongheart tend to think I am exaggerating his capacity for harm. They see him lounging like a kindly, white polar bear on the rug, begging for pets and making goo-goo eyes. His smile is famous. Since he was a pup, Strongheart has had his own unique and goofy expression of joy, which he uses to greet me when I have been gone for a long time. He smiles a "people smile," which makes him look remarkably like Elvis Presley. Then he tilts his huge head from side to side, high-steps with his front feet, and wiggles from stem to stern. He is now one hundred thirty pounds, and if you are on the back end of that wiggle, you can get knocked over inadvertently.

No one in my close circle of friends has seen Strongheart when he has become something else. A week ago, a friend came to visit and met Strongheart for the first time. This man is a wildlife veterinarian, and he knew without a doubt who Strongheart was the moment he met him. "I would far sooner go into a pen with an alpha wolf than with this dog," he told me, as Strongheart placed his paw over his shoe and sagged down next to him with deep sigh.

When I asked my friend what I should do, he paused for only a moment. Then he looked at me and held my eyes with his. "Strongheart is with you for a reason. He's come for something. You need to learn the lessons he has to teach you . . . and

I would suggest you learn them as quickly as possible. You need to put up an eight-foot fence, and you need to keep him away from any situation where he could do harm to others, or from any people who could make stupid mistakes around him. Susan, can you do that for him?"

Can you do that for him? For now — taking this aching walk only one day at a time — I have decided that I will try my best for Strongheart. And so I still take him for glorious off-lead runs, and he charges off across the pastures like a big gazelle with Arrow hot on his tail. But he wears a basket muzzle on his face and a shock collar around his neck. Strongheart will turn away from any temptation with one word and is the best behaved dog for miles. I watch his face carefully, to make sure in my very soul that his constrictions and restrictions have not eaten away his spirit. So far, they have not. He smiles big and often, even through the muzzle — a rig my friends call Strongheart's Hannibal Lechter outfit.

Our fences are getting higher, and the signs around our yard have gotten more menacing: "Keep Out." "White Dog — EXTREMELY Dangerous." Two strings of hot-wire top our fence of logs and wire mesh, not because Strongheart will attempt to get out, but because on two occasions recently, people have attempted to reach over and pet him even as he roars and peels his lips back in a horrific snarl. When Strongheart meets new neighbors while we are out walking — neutral territory in Strongheart's mind — they ask, "What's the muzzle for? He seems like a big baby to me." And I say, "He has a big, big mouth. It's better to be safe."

I say this knowing that neither Strongheart nor I — that none of us — are completely safe, not in our lives, not in our good intentions. And I dance across a tightrope of irony every moment of every day. Because while Strongheart has brought me a level of inner safety I never knew before, he has also brought me a new kind of fear — not for my own safekeeping but for his and for others'. Paradoxically, I have traded one fear for another.

Last night after I had written these words, I remembered a dream. I have spoken of it before, my dream of the bird-legged Great Goddess mummy. I still have not sorted all the pieces to this dream, nor have I tried hard to fit a particular meaning to it. Out of respect for my own soul, I don't rush these things. What I remembered last night was that the discovery and safekeeping of the Goddess's remains are not the only important elements in that dream. My finding and hiding of the Goddess mummy is undertaken in the setting of a devastating war and political coup in my country. In my dream, Nazis have overtaken the world, and all the Earth is desolate and burning. Armed units of young, fair-haired troopers are coming to take over each town.

In my dream, I have hidden the Great Goddess in my room, under my bed. Then comes a sequence in which I am outside, surrounded by the troopers, and they are laughing at me maniacally and threatening me with rape and torture, which will happen "when they come back." I don't know when they are planning to come back, but I know it is soon, very soon.

As I stand in the center of this circle of mockery and scalding evil, I am stunningly fearless. They would have taken me then, but close at my side is Strongheart. I tell them they will have to get past my dog to get to me. The leader grins hugely and says, "We'll just shoot him." I spit back, "You'd better shoot true because, believe me, you'll only have one chance." Strongheart growls low, facing each one of them with the look that had stopped my friends in their tracks when he was only a gangly puppy, and the troopers hesitate and turn away, grumbling. They leave threatening to return, but I know that as long as I keep Strongheart in my house with me, I am safe, and the Goddess is safe.

I do not know yet who the dream Goddess is, nor do I know who Strongheart represents. This is my task — to discover and know the Strongheart who is inside of me and part of me, and to recognize where the dog Strongheart begins and I leave off. This is perhaps the greatest hurdle I must leap to keep him safe — the hurdle of my own projections. We walk together in the winter snow, his paw prints more than half the size of my own tracks, and I promise him I will do my best to keep him away from harm and to find a vessel of security deep and true within myself so that he can stop shouldering this burden for me. He looks at me with the same eyes of adoration he turned upon me years ago as an airsick puppy, and I see him grin an Elvis Presley smile behind the cross wires of his muzzle.

Unclaimed Relations

SOULFUL MIRRORS, SACRED PROJECTIONS

Sometimes someone actually appears in our waking lives upon whom we project a part of the dream of who we could become.... They attract us with a promise — a potential to heal us — which we either correctly intuit or miscast upon them.

— Jean Shinoda Bolen, *Crossing to Avalon*

Years ago, I met a woman who introduced me to her tiny Pomeranian and told me, "He's depressed. Everyone forgot his birthday." Coincidentally, it was the woman's own birthday. The dog acted as a mirror to the depression she herself felt. It struck me at that time just how much we project onto our animal companions. They make marvelous objects for projection. Because of their silence and language, they cannot protest loudly in a way that human objects of our projection can.

I use the terms "mirror" and "projection" in the particular ways these concepts have defined themselves in my own life. By "mirror," I mean those things outside of us that reflect back to us who and what we are. For instance, I have a pretty calm and well-balanced family of animal companions right now, but that was not always the case. I have had my share of agitated, fearful, sickly, and what one might term neurotic animals partner with me over the years. I am comforted to see that my current animal family members are so peaceful and content. They are mirroring my own life right now. They validate my own experience of life as it is today, and how I am today.

By "projection," I mean those things inside of us that we bestow onto others — for good or ill — those things we own but do not claim for ourselves, like love, power, control, and beauty. Projections are those parts of our lives we are not living now but to which our souls are calling us. They include aspects of ourselves that are beautiful and strong, and also aspects that we call "shadow" and do not wish to know. Our souls are curious things, far more interested in our self-knowing than in our self-improvement. They call on us to recognize and to claim both our light and our darkness, and will not let us rest in peace until we do so.

Projections are often aspects of ourselves that we need to heal but are not attending to. If we fear or refuse to take ownership of this promise of healing, we tend to miscast these unclaimed aspects of our lives upon others, offering our love or our disdain to those others who we have burdened with parts of ourselves we are not yet willing or able to carry. The woman with the "uncelebrated birthday dog" very clearly needed healing herself. She was asking her little dog to carry a sorrow for her, and was offering her dog the nurture and acknowledgment she most likely denied herself in a hundred different ways every day. We all do this. It is hard to carry all the complexities and conundrums of being human, and it is human nature to put some of those challenges onto others for a time, until we are strong enough to claim them back and integrate them as we mature to greater wholeness.

Strongheart carries on his shoulders a heavy miscast burden of empowerment and safety. He carries this not only for me but for others who know him, and the truth of that comes out in statements that my friends and I make to each other: "Boy, when that jerk started cursing at me, Strongheart should have been there." Or, "I saw that guy hit his dog. I'd have liked to see him try that with Strongheart." Or, as I said to a friend whose house had been burglarized: "I'll loan you Strongheart."

We live in fearful, insane times. People can get shot just for driving down the highway in the wrong place at the wrong time, or for inadvertently offending a stranger. I know there is a kernel in me that is angry about this. No, not angry — furious. I am bloody screaming furious about what I read in the newspapers and what I hear and see going on in the world around me. I tell myself sometimes that I am too small to carry that much ferocity and rage and the insecurity it spawns, and yet my soul knows that it is right and proper to not only carry it but to embody it and own it. Until I am able to do that, Strongheart will carry it, and carry it at peril to his own existence. In our culture, it is more acceptable to be an angry and outraged person than to be an angry, outraged dog. Arnold Schwarzenegger gets applauded on screen for keeping the peace in ways that draw blood. Strongheart can be legally destroyed for it.

I remember my dream and how I stood fearlessly in the circle of evil, almost wishing for a confrontation. I am ashamed to say that it is not a feeling I have known only in my dreams. More times than I can count, or than I would care to admit to, I have felt a belligerent kind of antagonistic

pride in having Strongheart at my side, muzzle on his face.
I've seen people stopping to whisper to themselves and
exclaim at his sheer size, and at the message that muzzle
silently transmits: Watch out! We do not suffer fools.

Part of Strongheart's immense presence in my life has to
do with the process of reclaiming my own miscast projections. The whisper of his soul to mine asks that I claim my
empowerment, strength, ferocity, anger, and ability to create
a sense of safety for myself in an insane world. These are all
parts of myself that I can and need to become, for both our
sakes.

There are other things that the world and all our relations
desperately need us to reclaim. Things we may not think we
are worthy or courageous enough to own, to make manifest,
and to make present now for ourselves: love of self, healthy
pride, personal worth, self-nurture, compassion, openness to
the grace of God, transformation...the list is endless.

Would Strongheart turn into a gentle golden retriever if
I were to claim my own safety and power and anger? Sheesh,
no. He is who he is. But when I do my part, it will clear up
some of the stickiness between us. This stickiness takes many
forms in relationships involving projection. Here is one
small example: I have a friend who is handsome and bright
and saturated with a special artistic talent that is huge and
enviable. He is recognized among his colleagues and peers as
a gifted one. But he cannot yet claim the majesty of his gift.
Around me, he makes himself small, and makes me too big.
His gift is not as developed as my writing gift is, he says, nor
has he gotten a similar level of acclaim. Both of these things
are completely untrue. He is more recognized and celebrated

in his field than I am in mine, by far. This dynamic, in which he refuses to claim his own authority and accomplishment, makes me feel uncomfortable in his company any time we discuss our work. His self-imposed smallness feels false and at times even annoying.

On the day he becomes the talent he is, in his very bones and blood, I will not change. I will not morph into a waitress, or a writer of comic strips or mystery novels. But there will be a cleanness and wholeness between us when the stickiness of his projection melts off me. There will be a new world of potential in our interaction.

Similarly, on the day that I own the qualities I have miscast onto Strongheart — that is, when I feel the same sense of power, size, and pride walking alone as I feel when he is at my side — he will not change. He will not morph into a teddy bear. But I will see new potential in our relationship, potential that I am unaware of now.

How do I know this? Because sometimes I sit with Strongheart at night in front of the hissing glow of the propane heater and put my forehead against his snow-white brow, and something mysterious and true and huge passes between us. There is an indentation there in his brow that curves perfectly into the slope of my own forehead, just above my eyes, and we fit together like puzzle pieces. And sometimes when we come together like that, I look down into his eyes, all foggy around the edges and out of my focus, and I know that his face is mine, mine his. I know in those moments that our journey together is one journey, as *all* journeys are the One journey, and the possibilities are infinite.

A Practice

Do this exercise when you have plenty of time to play with it and your distractions are few. It comes in two parts. Please don't read Part Two until you have completed Part One. (I suspect that you are already hurrying along to see what Part Two is — that is what I would do, anyway. Don't worry, this activity will still work if you read ahead. But it is much more wonderful if you treat yourself and wait.)

PART ONE

Take yourself outside, with a journal or just a slip of paper, to the most beautiful place you know. Wander for as long as your heart calls you, giving thanks for this place and asking its consent to be there. As you meander, look for something that attracts you strongly. It may be a plant, the sky, water, a flower, a slug, a bird — anything that really catches your attention in a good way. Follow that attraction and spend time sitting with or near this bit of creation that has attracted you so positively. Slow down. Breathe. Breathe again. Do this as a gift to yourself.

When you've soaked up just about all the good feelings you can from this being that has called to you, complete this statement on paper: "I really enjoy/love (what you were attracted to) because it is _____."

Before you choose to end this process, be sure to thank whatever it is that has called to you for offering its help and insight. All creation thrives on being appreciated. Appreciation is an energy we send out that is healing and affirming to everything it lands upon. It is a gift you can offer, and should offer, to anyone or anything that relates genuinely to you, and nature cannot be anything but genuine.

PART TWO

Now, take the sentence you wrote in Part One and change the first part of the sentence to: "I enjoy/love *myself* because I am _____." Leave the rest of the sentence as you've already written it.

This exercise, devised by ecopsychologist and teacher Michael Cohen, will work every time. Even though I know both parts of this exercise, I can still go out, find what calls to me, and find qualities in it and myself that I have not yet claimed, projections that I am inclined to put onto nature or other people. Cohen has this to say about it: "You are nature: This revised sentence 'tricks' your language and reason senses to become conscious of your inner nature. Can you validate that the changed sentence describes some aspect of yourself?"[1]

Watch any tendency you may have to push away the good qualities this activity confers upon you. Say you found the words "colorful" and "energizing" to describe your special something in Part One, and therefore to describe yourself in Part Two. You may find it difficult to see yourself as colorful or energizing, but your unease is itself instructive. Perhaps even more than these qualities themselves, your inclination to feel uncomfortable about them can provide wonderful reflections and new perceptions about yourself and your relationships. Pay attention to these feelings, give witness to them on paper. Writing down your feelings, senses, and insights about this exercise will make it that much more a part of you.

Number 10

This is not a long story, because I did not know Number 10 long or well enough to fill many pages with my memories of him. Actually, I did not know him at all. I never had the honor of meeting him before he died. What I know of him comes from a couple of photographs and from the words of those who did know him for a short time. He lives on inside of me in part because he was a wolf, and no wolf or wolf-dog has crossed my path who has not shaken the ground of my life in a deep, deep way. I credit wolves — in particular the one I call Gaia — with helping me heal from cancer. Wolves have sparked my interior landscape for years. Number Ten sparked my living world briefly and profoundly. This is his story.

I am sitting at a dinner table in a firelit cabin just outside
of Yellowstone Park. It is 1996, and Canadian wolves have
just been released into Yellowstone after having been system-
atically exterminated from the park more than thirty years
ago. The initial fourteen wolves have not been free from
their pens for long, perhaps only weeks, before I arrive to
speak with the biologists involved in the wolf restoration
project. My friend Renee, who organized this informal dinner, pours the wine and passes a bread bowl around. The
biologists are telling me about one particular wolf.

"Number 10 is a real confident guy. He was the first one out of the Rose Creek pens, but he waited in the forest nearby for his mate and her daughter to come out. And they took their time.

"When we came up over the bluff by the pens, suddenly he was behind us on the ridge, so close! He started howling. There he was, standing behind the line of us, just facing us and howling. Unbelievable."

I recall my earlier conversation with Mark Johnson, the project veterinarian. He had also described the incident: "There were about nine of us who were going up to the pens that morning. We were bringing deer carcasses to put outside the pens to lure the wolves out. Snow was falling in large flakes, coming down so thick and heavy we could barely see in front of us. We walked single file into the woods, then dropped down into a little creek drainage just before the pens. When we climbed up the other side, we could see animals running in the pens, even though the gates had been opened for a couple of days. We expected all the wolves to still be in the pens, because that's what had happened when we opened the pens earlier for the Crystal Creek pack. The wolves were just too wary to leave.

"So, with all our intention out in front of us, suddenly we hear this howling immediately behind us. We were caught totally off guard. I ran back, retracing my steps up the hill, and there, standing up on the open hilltop, was the shadowy figure of a wolf through that falling snow. It was eerie. It was clearly Number 10. I knew him through his energy — through the intensity and confidence of that animal.

"He howled at us, mournfully at first. Then he barked and

sort of hopped on his back legs, swishing his tail. Well, the response of the group was instant panic. We realized that Number 10 was telling us to stay away from his two females, Number 9 and her daughter, Number 7. We dropped the carcasses in the ravine and left quickly through a frozen marsh of spindly pine. The whole time, Number 10 was paralleling our tracks, keeping high up on the slope but matching our pace, as though he was chasing us off. We were all quite shaken. We felt him. And we also felt a bit sheepish. If we had had tails, they would have been between our legs."

The biologists go on: "He's just so damn bold. Not aggressive. Just bold. You know, we worry about him. Just the other day, we said, 'There's a piece of lead out there somewhere with his name on it.' We're afraid he will be too confident about showing himself to people. He doesn't have any fear."

I am an infrequent drinker, and one glass of white Zinfandel has made me delightfully gay. My voice is a little louder than normal when I ask why they have chosen to number the wolves instead of naming them. In the uncomfortable silence that follows, my gut sense — even a bit dulled as it is — is that I have asked a stupid question that broadcasts my sentimentality and puts on neon blinking signs to advertise my embarrassing lack of professionalism. But the wine invites me to forgive myself, so I do, and I wait for their answers with a lilting smile on my lips. The biologists and their wives look at one another. One responds, "This is an experimental group of animals. The survival of one is not as important as the survival of the group. We see them as a group."

The stars were blazing in their eyes only seconds before as they spoke of Number 10, and I don't buy this "see-them-as-a-group" thing for a minute. As the table is cleared and the gathering moves into the small living room, a young wife pulls me aside. Beautiful and earnest, she touches my arm with fingers as light as feathers. "They are attached to these animals. They know they will lose some. It is inevitable. And it is so, so painful to consider. How much harder might that loss be if they were given names?" I told her I didn't know. Would it really be easier to lose one if it had been given only a number?

Later, after all the others leave, one biologist remains. The fire burns bright, and he talks about the wolves with his mouth, yes, but more so with his eyes. He is using his wine glass to punctuate his sentences, and his voice shines with emotion and energy. He tells me that whenever the weather allows, he flies the tracking plane to check out the telemeter readings on the wolves' radio collars, and he doesn't relax until he has found Number 10's signal strong and well. "Every time that signal comes in, we all sigh in relief. Yeah...the Big Guy." His voice trails off and I flash to a mental image of fresh wolf tracks, the guttural mutter of a small plane engine, and the blue shadow of a wing sweeping over the snow.

Weeks pass. Number 10 and his mate, Number 9, have moved up out of the park into Red Lodge, Montana, evidently looking for a place to den. On a fine May morning I am on the phone with Renee, whose award-winning poster of a Yellowstone wolf will be the cover of my first book, *Animals as Teachers and Healers*. The sound of her voice on the line — flat, distracted — startles me, and I feel my heart begin to thud. I ask her what has happened, and she tells me that only moments ago, the tracking plane picked up a "terminal" signal from Number 10's collar. It means the collar is not moving. They will immediately go look for it — and him.

That afternoon, Renee calls to tell me that his collar has been found in a creek. And not too long after, Number 10 is found dead in the creek as well: shot and skinned, except for the hide on his huge feet. I imagine him under the frigid water, bloody and naked but for his thick fur socks. I hang up the phone and weep for him, and for all the wolves — those living in my heart and those fighting for life on hostile lands — who I love with a sacred passion.

It seems to me that Number 10's story has been ended before it began. And yet no story ever ends, really. It just stitches itself somehow into a piece of the fabric of yet another story that is still becoming. And so Number 10's story takes a different twist.

Number 10's mate, Number 9, who has denned and borne Number 10's pups, will go on in the coming years to become the most celebrated wolf of the Yellowstone Recovery project. A legendary wolf, she will raise robust and bold litters of future young who will become many of the alpha wolves of new packs. Her blood runs strong in a great number of the wolves in Yellowstone today.

A poster of Number 10 hangs on the wall near my desk. He is running free, with his blazing yellow eyes on the camera and his huge tongue flapping like a windsock. I have told Number 10's story many, many times. I have not written of him since I wrote about the Yellowstone wolves in the final

chapter of *Animals as Teachers and Healers.* In the writing of
this story again now, Number 10 comes back to me. The
phone call that told of his death comes back to me, and I feel
my throat catch and my hands go loose. The years between
us fade away. I ask myself what his death has meant to me,
as I have asked this question many times and will continue
to ask it in the years to come.

Over these brief years much has changed in my life, and
in the world around me. It is time to ask myself what messages Number 10 has for me today. And he does have them,
there's no question. I know this because as I sat down to
write a completely different story, Number 10 began spilling
his bold, big-footed self onto the page. And this morning,
when I drew my daily Animal Card, it was Wolf. Story memories return when they have something new to tell us. When
a memory like this taps our shoulder, it is important that we
turn and listen.

When Number 10 came back to me this morning, the
first thing I did was to take my fingers off the computer keys
and rest my hands in my lap. My eyes went to the green trees
outside, and I took a long, full breath. I lit the scented candle
on my desktop. I took a few brief centering moments to
simply let Number 10 know that I "heard" him. In this quiet
place of mind, I began writing again.

Number 10's loss was a catalyst for me, a torch that
helped light the way to the completion of my first book. At
that time, I was writing for him and for the transpersonal
wolf — the sacrificial wild — inside of us that often remains
feared and mistrusted. In the eyes of the Biologist of the
Waving Wine Glass who loved Number 10 — and I know

that "love" is the true word for what I saw on his face as he spoke of him — I saw a vision of "wild" as a brilliant light: wild as passion, as consummate joy, and as boldness in the best sense.

Now it is eight years since I wrote of Number 10. It is cloudy outside my window, and the rain runs like silver wrinkles on the face of the glass. Today, this particular retelling of Number 10's story awakens a paradox I have been sensing about the concept of naming or labeling something. I ask myself, Who am I? and I come up with a slew of naming labels: writer, daughter, woman, cancer survivor. I read what I have written here, strike out some words, add others, read it again.

Number 10 . . . Number 10. Who was he? Names and labels are practical and necessary in the world we have created for ourselves. And yet something low in the center of my belly, curved moonlike in a sliver of nose and tail, cautions me that we often sacrifice chunks of truth in the pursuit of practicality. Number 10 tells me that the truth of what I know of him — and of myself — is nameless, wordless. He trots across my writing screen with his plumed tail up, asking me to remember this truth as I write with black words on white background — abstract ink tracks that frame but fragment whole truth.

Again my fingers rest on the keys for a moment before I continue casting letters onto the page. I believe that Number 10 has come back to me this morning to remind me of the dualistic nature of names and words, even as I sit paradoxically writing a book made up of nothing but names and words. Number 10 sniffs curiously at my words and cautions me to write mindfully, reverentially, and with awareness, daring me to find a way to let the truth show through the letters. All those years ago, I had felt that the biologists had somehow slighted Number 10 — and all the project wolves — in not granting them the dignity of a name. Today, I remember that long ago, the word for God was a series of unpronounceable letters, because the true name of the Holy One is beyond words.

Nameless Relations

UNNAMING THEM

Most of them accepted namelessness with the perfect indifference with which they had so long accepted and ignored their names. Whales and dolphins, seals and sea otters consented with particular alacrity, sliding into anonymity as into their element. ... Cattle, sheep, swine, asses, mules, and goats, along with chickens, geese, and turkeys, all agreed enthusiastically to give their names back to the people to whom — as they put it — they belonged....

The insects parted with their names in vast clouds and swarms of ephemeral syllables buzzing and stinging and humming and flitting and crawling and tunneling away. As for the fish of the sea, their names dispersed from them in silence throughout the oceans like faint, dark blurs of cuttlefish ink, and drifted off on the currents without a trace.

None were left now to unname, and yet how close I felt to them when I saw one of them swim or fly or trot or crawl across my way or over my skin, or stalk me in the night, or go along beside me for a while in the day. They seemed far closer than when their names had stood between myself and them like a clear barrier: so close that my fear of them and their fear of me became one same fear. And the attraction that many of us felt, the desire to feel or rub or caress one another's scales or skin or feathers or fur, taste one another's blood or flesh, keep one another warm, that attraction was now all one with the fear, and the hunter could not be told from the hunted, nor the eater from the food.

This was more or less the effect I had been after. It was somewhat more powerful that I had anticipated, but I could not now, in all conscience, make an exception for myself. I resolutely put anxiety away, went to Adam, and said, "You and your father lent me this — gave it to me, actually. It's been really useful, but it doesn't exactly seem to fit very well lately. But thanks very much! It's really been very useful."

It is hard to give back a gift without sounding peevish or ungrateful, and I did not want to leave him with that impression of me. He was not paying much attention, as it happened, and said only, "Put it down over there, O.K.?" and went on with what he was doing.

One of my reasons for doing what I did was that talk was getting us nowhere, but all the same I felt a little let down. I had been prepared to defend my decision. And I thought that perhaps when he did notice he might be upset and want to talk. I put some things away and fiddled around a little, but he continued to do what he was doing and to take no notice of anything else. At last I said, "Well, goodbye, dear. I hope the garden key turns up." He was fitting parts together, and said, without looking around, "O.K., fine, dear. When's dinner?"

"I'm not sure," I said. "I'm going now. With the —" I hesitated, and finally said, "With them, you know," and went on out. In fact, I had only just then realized how hard it would have been to explain myself. I could not chatter away as I used to do, taking it all for granted. My words must be as slow, as new, as single, as tentative as the steps I took going down the path away from the house, between the darkbranched, tall dancers motionless against the winter shining."

— Ursula K. Le Guin, "She Unnames Them"

As a child, I named every living thing that crossed my path. Never once did I consider the consequences of names, or even that there might possibly be consequences. A name was an honor bestowed, a blessing granted. If you had a name, you *were*.

Le Guin's bold look at the other side of naming serves as a profound counterbalance to that idea. A name grants something, yes, but in many cases, it steals away more than it grants.

A week ago, I stood in front of a university classroom beside a visiting great-horned owl and a small, delicate German shepherd. The owl was permanently injured and would never fly again. The dog, Journey, was used in therapy programs. Both came with their Humane Society guardian. With a stick of dried cedar, I smudged the room with a light smoke. A student turned the fluorescent lights down. Wafting the tails of smoke into the air, I asked the students to unname these animals. To take away the names, good and bad, we had bestowed upon them without consent. The class fell silent. The owl turned his head and looked into the faces of the students with a studied deliberation. Journey panted, then rolled into a luxurious stretch, toes flexing. A short time later when the lights came up, I asked the students to share what, if anything, they had sensed.

"I felt my responsibility to protect them."

"I felt the individual in them. They are both really cool!"

"Without their names, there was more there."

"They became sacred."

Naming is both a blessing and a curse. It is fine to bestow names upon things. We need to name things in order to speak to each other and make some amount of sense. But let's not lose the power of namelessness. It, too, is our birthright.

A Practice

In all the world, we are the only creatures who feel the need to name things. Getting beneath a creature's name is a beautiful and powerful exercise.

Take some moments in silence to sit before an animal or plant you have good feelings for. To help yourself get into the mind-state for unnaming this particular being, you might want to create a small ritual — using smudge, for example, or lighting a candle, or singing a short honoring song. Take a series of centering breaths and bring yourself as much as possible into the present moment. Give this process the respect it is due. It is an enormous gift to bestow a name, and also to remove one.

Bring the creature you have chosen into your awareness. You may do this with eyes open or closed. See if you can get a sense of the being behind the name. In erasing its name, do you see this being any differently? Do you have any sense that by releasing your judgments, you may be allowing this being to see you differently? Is there any change in the connection between the two of you? Sitting in the silence, go further and unname yourself. Who are you behind your name?

If this process feels valuable to you, take it one step further. Seek out something or someone, some animal or insect or plant that you have negative feelings for — a spider, poison oak, a rat, a slug — I'm naming some of the more commonly disenfranchised souls here — and do this same process. In an honorable way, unname them. Do you sense anything different or new? Any change in attitude or perspective about either them or yourself?

Writing down your observations or sharing them with a friend will help to embed the power of this process into your daily life.

River Elk

It was to be the most glorious of summers. All my prayers for the right place, the right work, the right time converged the day I signed the lease for the River House. I had just sold my home, the home that had burned to cinders and that I had rebuilt over the course of a year. My divorce was finalized, my new book partly done. I had a new sweetheart, Fritz, and my passion for life was flowing like the snowmelt that had just begun running down the Tetons.

The house itself was modest, a fifties-vintage cabin with little character that had seen better years. I referred to it as "cozy," but in truth, it was tiny and cramped, with bedrooms that must have been designed before the creation of queen-sized beds. The back porch had partially caved in, the

kitchen stove was home to several generations of mice, and the gravel driveway was a maze of teeth-rattling potholes and ruts that turned into lakes and rivers after a moderate rain.

But the front window faced the Grand Tetons, and the kitchen in back looked out over a meandering trout stream that flowed between high cottonwood and willows. Between the cabin and the mountains was nothing but the Snake River, flowing in undulating channels and carving out an ancient strand of river bottom. The setting was as close to paradise on Earth as anything I have ever seen before or

since. That the cabin was there at all, and that it was available to us, was a miracle. I imagine you could count the
small, history-laden cabins that remained along the Snake
River in Jackson Hole on one hand. Our neighbors were all
millionaires and billionaires, their houses not houses at all but
huge estates with grand names and entry gates made of massive logs, iron, or stone. We never met any of them. Next
door to us, an 8,500-square-foot log and rock estate with its
own man-made stream that you actually could switch on and
off was under construction. The builders of this estate property controlled the general lease on our tiny cabin, which sat
just out of sight behind a stand of spruce and cottonwoods,
and they were wanting to rent it out for at least six months.

I signed the lease papers on the first of April, near giddy
with joy, and the very next day we began moving boxes into
the place we christened the River House. The porches were
still sagging under the weight of old winter snow, and the
trees around the place were ashen colored and bare. The
Snake River out our front door was at a low trickle, receiving just a fraction of the snowmelt that would be in full
cascade by May. Through the gray and spindly mish-mash
of cottonwood twigs and willow bushes, our other new
neighbors slipped past us in full and stunning view as we
unpacked box after box: eagles, owls, deer and elk, moose,
two brown bears, muskrats and beavers, porcupines, coyotes,
delicate-legged cranes, geese by the hundreds, and endless
flocks of returning songbirds.

I filled up a half dozen bird feeders twice a day to keep
up with the throngs of chickadees and grosbeaks, nuthatches
and flickers, hummingbirds and titmice. A family of seven

baby chipmunks moved into the woodpile just outside our back door and stuffed the pockets of their cheeks with sunflower seeds scattered by the birds.

God was blessing me, I told myself, for all the hard inner work I had done reconciling myself to the house fire of the previous year. How generous all the spirits were to bring me to this magnificent place in which to complete my book and begin my new life with my new love. I moved to the cabin humble and grateful, knowing that it was a sign of affirmation that I had done a good job and was on Creator's spiritual "A-list."

For the rest of the summer, it just got better. The trees budded, and goslings and otters floated by on the swollen river, which called to us day and night with a voice like strong, fresh wind. Cranes did their mating dances, wings outstretched and toes pointed, leaping into the blue mountain air. A baby boot-nosed bull moose nibbled on willow branches outside my office window, so close I could hear the leaves being pulled from the stems while I wrote at my small desk for hours and days that seemed endless, timeless.

The feathers that came to me on my river walks each day with the dogs were tantalizing. I found the fluffy breast feathers of ravens and owls, the tail feather of a bald eagle, the crisp wing feathers of geese and hawks and ducks. Our front porch became a tangle of driftwood and old bones. For each of the gifts I brought home from the abundant river, I gave thanks and left a gift in return: strands of my hair, a flower, a spontaneous song, a prayer.

And then on the twenty-third of August, on a warm night that held just the tiniest hint of fall, my grand and affirmative summer became completely perfect. In the still of the late night, under a canopy of summer stars, a bull elk trumpeted outside our bedroom window. His voice started low in his chest, rumbling up his neck in a hollow bellow that morphed into a high and breathy flute whistle as it left his lips. The sound of the rut — the seeding of new life — is a sound I seek out every fall, but this was the first time the sound ever came to find me. Always before, it had been me stealing quietly into the forest in hopes of finding the bulls, listening on the edge of night meadows for the sound that brings shivers up my spine and into my face and squeezes hot tears out of my eyes.

This night, the elk came to me, singing a circle around the River House, bellowing his love song until the black sky blended into dawn pearl. For all the symphony of sounds I had heard that summer, nothing touched the magic of his music. As the night sky faded, I heard his hooves crunch in the dry cottonwood leaves and fade into the morning toward the river. In the ensuing moments of predawn silence, I imagined he had come to me as a culmination of all the signs of affirmation I had received that summer. All were gathered to him, held by him, wrapped in the gift wrap of his voice and tied in ribbons of his presence.

When he returned near dawn the next day to serenade me again, I bolted from my bed to catch a glimpse of him. In the gray light, I saw him walking away from me, once more toward the river. His crown of antlers was fat as my arm at the base, held high on a neck thick and dark as a tree trunk — and no doubt as strong. He stepped high and deliberately, and his outstretched nose was humped and broad. How beautifully, how perfectly he suited his voice.

In the weeks to come, two more bull elk came to the river: one with a lyrical call of all flute notes and no chest bellows, and one square-bodied, stout fellow whose call was always discordant and off-key. In the night, we would hear the trio of bulls dueling for the herds of cow elk that were gathering all around us. At first the bugles would sound far from one another, then closer as the bulls marched forward to fight for the right to claim the cows. On still nights when the air carried the sound from the river up to the sky, we would hear the clack of their antlers crashing against one another, the sound of bone to bone.

During the daylight hours, mostly in the morning and at twilight, we would sometimes catch precious glimpses of the elk, both cows and bulls, hurrying along the dry river channels, anxious and excited with the energy of rut and breeding. Soon we realized that the off-key bull and the lyrical, fluting bull had lost the battle for the cows. The harems were in the custody of "our" bull — the deep-voiced, massive, crowned singer. It could be no other way. The fluting bull was smaller, younger. The off-key bull lacked that throaty resonance that signifies a huge-necked, mature, confident bull elk. The cows had chosen well.

On an evening walk I will never forget, we turned a bend on the riverbank and caught a view that lodged my breath in my heart. It was September, twilight hushing the sounds of the day. In front of my eyes, a peninsula of sand and grasses jutted out into the season-spent river. Gathered on that white sand, standing quietly among clumps of green bushes and yellow grass, twenty-four cow elk grazed under a sinking sun that splashed golden light across their backs. Between us and the cows marched the bull, our bull, strutting back and forth, nodding his antlers from side to side, stretching out his neck and face to shoulder level, and bellowing his song. His back, too, was lit with the golden light that poured from the autumn sky like honey. The whole world before me seemed to be wrapped in a circle of precious amber, and peace rose up from my heart and lodged in my throat. I wished instantly and fervently for that sight to never leave me, and it never has. I wrapped my arms around Fritz and sighed into his chest that life could get no better than this.

The next day, as though in direct response to my claim of perfection, our landlord called to deliver the news: The big estate next door was completed and sold, and the new owner had other plans for our little cabin. We had thirty days to move. Thirty days to pack up, to find a place that would rent to us with two dogs and a cat, and to put the River House behind us.

Both of us were struck speechless and numb. Normally, I go into high gear at times like this; my middle name is Can-Do. But this time, I collapsed inside and out and could do nothing. My feet felt weighted with river rocks, and I walked through the next week of shining autumn glory as though I were wading through mud. Fritz collected boxes, but I could not fill them. I could not lift up my hands in any effort that would take me away from my home on the river. They hung in clenched, hopeless fists from my arms and would not serve me. At night while I huddled under my covers — exhausted, miserable, sick — the river elk, our elk, would call hauntingly from the woods by the water, and I would weep and wonder how I could possibly leave him.

On Saturday morning two weeks after our landlord had told us we needed to move on, Fritz and I finished up an early oatmeal breakfast and headed out from the front door on a straight line toward the river. The air was clear and citrus-flavored, and the dogs were leaping like gazelles. I was in a bubble of misery that even the river could not burst, and so I did not notice at first that the cottonwood tree in front of me was draped with a hundred ravens. I did not notice the magpies whirling over me, or my dogs as they shifted from dancing to stillness. These things pierced me only when Fritz said, "Can you smell it?"

"Can you smell it?" Like a waft of black smoke, the scent enveloped us: thick, sweet, rank. Real time became dream-time, and we moved forward silently, like puppets on God's strings, pulled against our will to the edge of a sandy bank that dropped off to the river bottom. Above us the ravens hunched silent and wary. Below us, just there over the edge of the low bank, lay a tangle of massive branches.

No, not branches. Oh God. Antlers.

Sprawled in front of us, his neck twisted harshly, his huge rack of horns impaled point-first into the dirt, lay the river elk, dead. The four of us froze in silence. In slow motion the dogs approached him, crouching, and extended their noses to touch his golden back. Arrow whined and licked him softly. I slid down the bank and dropped to my knees beside him and extended my hands, my leaden hands that had stopped serving me, to touch his neck. It was still warm. Sounds fell from our mouths as Fritz placed his hands on the white tips of the elk's antlers, but no words came to us. In those first moments of shock and denial, all we could do was murmur, sigh, gasp, and moan. When we could finally speak, we told ourselves that he must have been fatally gored in a battle with one of the other bulls.

We touched him everywhere, from his glassy dull eyes to the curve of his sable-colored thigh. There was not a mark on him. He was sleek, fat, shiny, massive. Urine soaked his shaggy mane, and I felt its stickiness on my hands. That rancid anointment had been a signal of his pride and his power, the cologne of the breeding bull, the intoxication of his cows.

The birds loomed above us, impatient and suspicious. Now, my legs and hands moved freely. My mind cleared. What to do? First, pray. Then, open him up for the birds. Fritz headed back to the cabin to fetch an ax and my ceremonial pipe and some sage. I sat in tears, rocking and stroking the velvet nose of this one whose voice had carried me on a magic carpet of sound through the most picture-perfect summer of my life. I could not leave him, I told myself, and so he had left me.

His body was bent in a wrenched and awkward pose. It looked as though he had fallen off the shallow embankment head first and never moved again. Instinct commanded my hands as it had years before, when I prepared and tended the body of my father for the coming of the hearse. I grabbed the bull's feet and tugged, trying to roll him onto his side so that I could ease his antlers from the dirt and lay him out in a figure of repose. His deadness resisted me, hundreds of pounds of nonresponsive flesh and bone, but gravity was on my side. He finally turned and settled so that his neck and his trunk were facing the same way.

That was when I found the small, bloodless hole up near

his back. Why I did what I did next, I do not know. My hands reached for the wound and then into it, fingers coursing up into his body, while my mind said, How deep? How deep does a gore wound go? I felt the splinter of a bone against my hand and automatically wrapped my fingers around it and pulled. My hand rose up in front of my face holding not a bone, but the broken shaft and razored point of a metal arrow. Blood dripped from its hollow core. My eyes widened in horror. It was not the world that had taken him away from me, but a poacher on these private lands. Someone had watched for this bull, for these antlers, for this head.

I shivered and looked into the trees around us. Surely, surely, he was there. Surely he had stalked our elk as he stumbled his way through the trees to collapse and die directly in front of our cabin. I looked at Strongheart laying quietly, watchfully, a few feet away. My devoted and fearless guardian, Strongheart would defend me and defend this spot against anyone. I would not give up the river elk.

When Fritz returned, we smudged the body of the elk with sage and tied prayer ties to his ankles. We gathered dried flowers and foxtails into a bundle. I loaded and offered my pipe, sending prayers for the river elk's soul journey and gratitude for his voice and his magic. With ax and butcher knife, we split open his hide so that the birds could carry his spirit with them. And then in the end, we severed his head — that prized and regal head that had cost him his life — and dragged it back to the cabin with us.

That afternoon, with Strongheart in tow, I hurried back once more to the elk's body, carrying an old elk skull I had found along the river. I placed it at the elk's neck and then stepped back, taking a long, cleansing breath. The river elk lay with his skull head grinning, his feet sprouting the colors of the prayer wrappings, a bouquet of dying wild flowers and grasses over his heart. He was a spirit being now, and I stood still in wonderment at the look of him. It was not yet time to leave. I sat down near the bank and asked myself questions, deluding myself into thinking I knew the answers.

My first question was Why? Several answers came to me: He did this for me. I am not good enough. It is a sign. God has dropped you from her A-list. I have failed the test of this summer. Then, What was the test? Something is over, a new beginning is coming. Have you not felt it in the cold night winds of these weeks? You and your new love are crumbling, and your partnership will not last.

Because I did not know what else to do, I rose to leave. "Take me with you," I heard. I looked at the elk. "I did take you with me," I told him. "Your head is in my car. I'll clean it down to bone and keep it safe always. I'll honor your spirit."

"Take me with you." My body jolted up in sudden recognition. I knew exactly what I was being asked to do. Communion.

"I don't know if I can do this. I'll be sick."

In slow motion, my hands sweating cold, I crouched down by the river elk's gaping neck wound and tore off a small chunk of meat. Gagging, I put it in my mouth and swallowed hard. It tasted horrid. Metallic, gritty, greasy. My throat muscles constricted around the flesh and tried to send it back up. I swallowed again, gagged again, and then it was done.

Calling Strongheart to me, I turned away from the elk and hurried back to the cabin. It was finished. The summer, the elk — all of it. That night, my no-longer-uncooperative hands wrapped themselves around me like a comforting shawl, and in the morning I began to pack.

Coded Relations

INTERPRETING SIGN LANGUAGE

In times past, people understood and knew how to interpret
these portents and omens. . . . However, as technology expanded,
people became more and more isolated from their
connection to earth and their inner wisdom.

— Denise Linn, *The Secret Language of Signs*

I am a believer in signs and omens. My writing is full of reflections on the meaning of animal signs and messages. I believe that the Holy One has many words for us but speaks few of them in English. We were human long before we had formal words. I don't believe that the One waited for the development of spoken and written language to start talking to us. Since time began, humankind has listened to the words of the air, the stars, the animals, the moments of startling serendipity and has called these holy words "signs."

Words that we write and speak generally appear to be pretty clear-cut in their meaning. We even have books that tell us the precise meaning of all the words known to all people. And yet how often do we fail to communicate clearly and precisely with words, spoken or on paper? Who in her lifetime has not said, "That's not what I meant"? Who has not heard himself say, "I misunderstood you"?

If formal words can betray us so easily, how can we possibly translate correctly the coded language of signs? The truth is, we can't. We can only stumble around and play hit-and-miss. But these clumsy and humble efforts are seen by the One and cherished. To try and translate the code of signs is our job. It is what humans do. It is what all animals do. Animals are master sign readers. Nothing that crosses their path is dismissed. They read the language of air, water, fire, season, and time, and they interpret the messages at the places where these signs intersect.

We, too, interpret signs and have done so since our time began. But our sign reading comes with the blessing and the curse of consciousness. Our big minds offer big gifts and equally big stumbling blocks to our dance with sign language. One such stumbling block is our need to be right, our desire for an "exact" interpretation. We sense that a sign has crossed our path, our dreams, our inner eye, and we conclude that it has a specific meaning for us, limited in scope or time.

In just this past week of writing the story of the river elk, two beautiful examples of sign language have presented themselves to me. A friend found office space in the Black-hawk Office Building in our small town. The black hawk is one of her spirit guides. It was indeed the perfect space for her work. She rented it, and in the next few days her financial world and her health began unraveling just as the office lease monies were due. How could it have looked so right and then turned so suddenly into such a nightmare? Well, for my friend the answer was simple. She believed she had done something wrong. Have you ever had this feeling — this feeling that if only you had gotten things right then the chaos would not be happening (even if you have no clue what "right" might look like)?

Sign language is not a matter of right or wrong. Often it is a matter of timing. When Black Elk, the legendary Lakota holy man, was nine years old, he received a vision that he would lift up his people, that he would make the sacred tree at the center of the world bloom again. He died in despair, believing he had failed utterly. Yet the book that was written about Black Elk's life — *Black Elk Speaks,* by John Neihardt — has lived far beyond the old holy man and is now a classic in indigenous and religious literature. The story of Black Elk's life, told in his own words, has been a spiritual awakening for thousands of seekers. A half-century after his death, Black Elk is still fulfilling the vision he thought had died with him. He is lifting up the hearts and minds of the people, setting the sacred tree to flower.

Two days before my friend decided to let her office space go for the time being, a group of us was still helping her move into the place. My dear friend Tim was one of the box carriers, and helping my friend move into an independent work space was triggering deep callings of his own. Tim is the executive director of a small foundation that was whispering for a new name and a new home. As we stood in the middle of the office, surrounded by boxes and furniture and wall hangings, the word "RiverWind" surfaced among us of its own accord.

Tim has struggled with the word "RiverWind" for a decade. He felt it was his given spirit name, but at the same time, he never felt that he truly owned it. Only standing in the middle of my friend's office did he understand that it was the perfect name for his nonprofit foundation. The name was not for him personally, but it had been given for him to carry for those years so that it could find its home as the spirit name for his lifework as a facilitator of personal empowerment and deep community. It had been a matter of timing and trust for Tim to bring the name to its true home.

My friend's office was a perfect dream, a lovely vision. The universe was giving her an advance preview of what was to come, but not just yet. She had done nothing wrong. The hand of the Holy One reaching out to us is a loving hand, not a club wielded to smack us when we don't get it right. All messages are kind, even when they don't seem so at the time.

Another challenge to our reading of signs is the human quality of inflexible conviction. We must not become too sure in our translation of things as ephemeral as sign language. Sometimes illness means one thing, and sometimes another, and sometimes a cold is just a cold. Both the bugaboos of needing to be right and inflexible conviction reared up in my own reflections on the meaning of the life and death of my river elk.

At the outset, I imagined his trumpeting presence was a blessing and anointing of my hard winter of work and a productive summer of writing to come. But then I convinced myself that he had really come to the river to die for me, and that his death was timed to move me forward into a transition that I was unable to make on my own. These convictions left me feeling spiritually responsible for his death. I felt guilty and small and unworthy, as though his passing were that club in the hand of the Holy One, smashing me because I was just too weak and whiney to get up and get myself moving. Of these things I was convinced beyond doubt.

But I had it wrong. The club is in our hands alone, wielded against ourselves. And the timing of all things is in the hands of the Holy One. The reading of signs is a delicate and sacred business, not to be tainted with grandiosity. In truth, the life and death of the river elk were not about me. The Creator does not send and murder elk for my instruction. It is never all about me. Signs are indeed the voice of the Holy One, but the bearer of the message has a journey of its very own. My river elk lived and died the destiny he came here to fulfill, and it was not him but the moments of our crossing paths that sparked the whisper of a sign, of many signs, for me.

Imagine a circle and two lines crossing at the center. Each line is its own, given to itself, not sent or sacrificed for the other line. When the lines cross, a portal or gate is opened and activated and God begins whispering — or shouting, as the case may be. The truly humbling thing about this process of crossing lives and moments of sacred intersection is the mysterious orchestration of it all. I imagine it would have been far easier for the Holy One to say "Oh, say, it's time to kill that elk for Susan. Get that poacher ready" than to orchestrate an infinite number of meaningful crossings and convergences — none of which sacrificed or compromised my destiny, or that of the elk.

Seen in this way, I fulfilled my duty to the elk, and the elk to me. The poacher also fulfilled his duty and was as important a piece of the sacred fabric as any of us. All of us were given to each other at the place where the lines of our lives intersected. These coded messages released at the portal of confluence are sent out in sign language, so that each and every being has the opportunity to hear what it is meant to hear. How do I know this is true? I don't. I'm translating as best and as carefully as I can because I am human and am driven by my soul to do this. In my bones, I know that serendipity and coincidence are the soul's code.

I admit that I am no master at sign language. But mastery is not the point. When a mother sings a lullaby to her infant, something more than words is passing between them. Babies don't understand words, and lullabies are mostly in code, anyway ("Rockabye Baby, in the tree top...."?). A lullaby from a mother to a child is sign language, and the importance is not in the translation but in the tender, all-consuming love the singing reveals.

I believe that we are each loved enough to be sung lullabies by the Great Mother/Father. To seek to know the words and meanings of the lullaby is in my nature as a human animal, but precise translating is really only the frosting on the cake. The greater gift is to remember we are cradled and crooned to for life.

It has been a bit more than two years since my river elk died. I buried his head up to the base of his antlers under a tree on a friend's property, and he rested there for nearly eighteen months. During that time, I sank into a spiritual and physical maw that nearly swallowed me whole until it finally spit me out, clear again. Since then, I have returned to the memory of the river elk, which leaves me humbled and open and admittedly unsure, looking for new meaning. And I find it there, blossoming as the months and years pass. Yes, he signified an affirmation for me, and a transition. And he foreshadowed an intense and nearly fatal inner death I did not see coming at all. Yes, my romance disintegrated. Yet I was able to move on again and again and again, even at those times when my hands and heart would not serve me. I have visited his resting place by the river, and again the portal opened and the One whispered.

The head of the river elk came up out of the ground last spring, his skull the color of vanilla, clean and smooth as stone. Over my prayer altar he resides, and I look at him in this moment and can hear his unique, bellowing song. I had my old wedding ring melted down and one of his ivory teeth set into it. A hunting guide who saw the tooth said he had never seen one so tarnished and worn, that the elk who sported it must have been a grandfather, an ancient one. And so I am married in a sense to the meaning of him, still just beginning to tap into the sign language of our crossing paths, the lines that transect the sacred circle.

A Practice

We can invoke sign language by asking for it and by letting the universe know we are intending to listen. Nature is where I go to hear most clearly, and I invite you to do this, too. Here is a simple yet powerful process for inviting this kind of communication: First, select a question you have been struggling with. It can be anything from the sublime to the ridiculous. You might ask about the meaning of life, or you might ask about whether you should buy that new car, or give up eating sugar. Sit a while with this question and really get it soaking into your cells. Ruminate, muse, ponder.

Now, with focused attention, take this question into nature. Nature can be as big as a forest, or as small as your backyard. It really doesn't matter. What does matter is that you ask for help and guidance and permission to come before her with this question. As you ask, let yourself be attracted to a thing, a place, a trail — something in the area that is inviting to you. This sense of welcome or invitation is nature giving her consent and her attention to you. Follow and trust that attraction! Walk or sit with your question in mind. Open up to anything you see, feel, smell, sense.

If a twig calls to you, acknowledge it and enjoy it. If the wind is sweet, allow yourself to experience it on as many sensory levels as you can. Wind, for instance, is not just sound. It is touch, smell, balance, temperature, direction, taste. Repeat your question. Don't let your question drown out any signs that are being presented to you in the symphony of your senses. And don't let your question get lost, either. Balance the sensing and the asking. Remain in this place for as long as you are drawn to do so. For some, it may be an hour; for others, a few precious minutes.

Resist the urge to start translating if it overcomes you. It will be difficult sometimes. Before you leave, thank the place, the things, the moment, and do this with a full heart. You can now delve into the sign language this small quest has offered you in many ways.

You might want to write about what you saw and felt. You may choose to sit with it and just let your mind and body respond with ideas and sensations. I find it most helpful to take the experience to bed at night and just let it soak in wordlessly. You may find surprising insights into your question when you wake up the next morning. Or you may not. The point is not to become better interpreters, but better listeners. And to trust in the love of the lullaby.

Tarantulove

O ut of the corner of my eye I saw her, a tiny spider no bigger than a pea making her tentative way across the vast expanse of my bedcovers. Instantly, I went stiff. Her body was the color and size of a small pearl, her eight legs deep espresso brown. My ten-year-old face contorted at the sight of her, and I heard the shriek explode out of my lungs with the force of a whale spouting. By the time my mom arrived with a tissue and squashed her, I was close to hyperventilation. That night, I burned every light in my room and slept with the covers over my head.

I lived in a small factory town where tired streetlights burned away the light of the stars and yellow smog regularly obliterated the green hills standing not more than three miles from our tiny suburban house. The night of the terrible

spider massacre, I was burrowed deep in my bedcovers, reading my favorite book, *Understood Betsy*. It is the story of a
young city girl who finds herself suddenly sent to live with
distant relatives on a poor, northeast farm. Word for word, it
was the story of my secret childhood dream. But in my
dreams, Betsy never had to contend with bugs, particularly
spiders, no matter how remote her surroundings.

   That something as harmless as an innocent spider coming to visit in the peace of night should throw me into such
trembling paroxysms of fear and sleeplessness attests to the
powerful effect that horror movies and collective cultural
stupidity and bias had had on me by that tender age. I'm

certain I was not born afraid of spiders. As a youngster, I had never been harmed by a spider, nor by any other insect save a hapless honeybee that found himself under my bare and unaware foot.

My spider fear and countless other senseless fears I still harbor I absorbed from the body of my culture. Our societal myth about the danger of wild nature and her children — rats, bats, spiders, wolves, snakes, darkness, storms, silence — is an old one, well-secured in human hearts by the time the first settlers arrived in this country. I have written about this fear of wild Earth and wild kin in my first book, *Animals as Teachers and Healers,* but until recently I had never fully considered just how fully imprisoned I was by it. "What is not useful is vicious," wrote Puritan leader Cotton Mather. I had never heard those words as a child, but somehow, I had ingested them. That is exactly how I felt about spiders. They were of no use to me, so they were vicious.

My spider terrors did not diminish as I grew older. In fact, without my mother there all the time with a fly swatter or a paper towel in hand, my fears seemed to intensify and to make nights away from home almost unbearable. A spider on the ceiling or scuttling along a floorboard would mean a night without sleep, as I sat crouched in the covers, nearly crippled with the crazy fantasy that somehow the insect was searching for me, would find me, would — God forbid — crawl across me.

As I grew older it baffled and frustrated me no end that I was aware enough to recognize the immobilizing power of my phobia but not aware enough to influence it in the least. Telling myself I was being foolish, stupid, ridiculous, and childish was useless. There was simply no way my analytical brain could make contact with my body and convince it of anything. Grace and hope finally came to me in the form of a college psychology class, where I first read about a technique for phobia called "submersion," in which people face their phobia head on, even hands-on if need be. Not being patient by nature, I thought diving in seemed about the best option for facing my spider fears.

Large spiders were all the rage at that time as "pets," and every pet shop had its retail collection of both drab (cheap) and colorful (costly) tarantulas imprisoned in small glass tanks. On a Saturday afternoon marked by brilliant skies and crisp sunshine, I walked into a store and asked if I could hold one of the spiders. Perhaps I seemed like a composed, potential buyer to the skinny youngster behind the counter. I was far from it. It had taken me weeks of sleepless nights and nervous fits to get this far. My stomach was churning and my hands were as cold as icicles. Only the acute level of my desperation could have pushed me into the pet shop that day. I had decided that I would meet my fear where it lived by allowing a spider — a huge, huge spider — to speak to me through touch.

"Which one would you like to see?" the boy asked.

None of them, I thought. Not a single miserable one. "That big one — the one with the orange stripes on its legs," I answered in a voice that sounded hollow and far away.

Pulling down the small tank from the shelf, the boy began a long stream of talk as he slowly removed the screen lid and reached his hand down to the arachnid, who pulled away and hunched herself into a corner of her glass cell. She was a beautiful thing. I could see that even through my fear, which had enveloped me in a dreamy, surreal fog. Her hair was erect and shiny black. Bright orange bands the color of ripe pumpkins encircled her legs, which were nearly as large around as my pinky fingers.

The boy was soft-voiced and patient. He simply rested his hand, open and palm up, next to the tarantula and waited. "When I pass it to you, don't jerk away or try to fling it off. Don't blow on it, because it gets them mad. Don't poke it. You can pet it, but if it puts its front feet up, stop. That means it's getting upset. It won't bite or anything."

"It." I never like hearing an animal referred to as "it." His use of the impersonal pronoun inadvertently brought me into a weak alliance with the spider, forging the tiniest thread of a bond between us, just strong enough to keep my feet planted on the linoleum and to keep me from bolting out of the store.

The spider was beginning to uncurl herself, and looked to be about the size of my palm. With one feathery leg, she reached forward and touched the boy's hand. Soon, all eight feet were moving in the direction of his outstretched fingers, and then she was sitting quietly with the orb of her body centered in his palm. He slowly raised his hand up and extended it to me. I saw my own hand reach forward with no sense at all that it was connected to my arm, and as the boy tipped his hand up, I felt the first touch of the spider's sticky feet against my fingers. My body recoiled, but somehow my hand remained extended. I turned my face away from her and closed my eyes. More feather-weight feet touched my hand, then there was only stillness. Turning my face, I opened my eyes and I saw her snuggled down into the cup of my palm. "It likes the warmth," the boy said. "It'll start moving soon."

As though he had given her marching orders, she raised her body and began moving delicately toward my wrist, waving each leg slowly in the air like a curious antennae before resting it on my skin. My face seemed to be miles away from my arm, as though I were viewing this bizarre and unlikely event from outer space. Quiet pervaded my body. There was a curious rushing sound in my ears that drowned out all sound save for the occasional comments from the sales boy.

I watched, entranced, as she made her tentative way past my elbow, tickling the hairs on my arm as she went. My focus was entirely upon her, upon the sleekness of her, and upon the soul of her. At my armpit, she paused and waved her two front legs, clearly at the crossroads of a choice: Down to the torso, or up to the face? My fear gave way before a flood of simple enchantment and childlike wonder. So close to the spider, I found it suddenly impossible not to see the personhood that resided with such dignity there. She waited and stroked her back leg thoughtfully, a spider-person at a turn in the road. What do to? Ah, well, why not the high road? With a slight shift, she spoke to all of her legs and each one turned in unison, aiming up, up over my shoulder to touch the thin skin of my neck underneath my hair.

"Ick! Oh, man, it's going to walk across her face! Gross!" Lost in my enchanted trance, I did not realize we had attracted a small, encircling audience. "Eeeyoo — What does it feel like?" someone asked.

"Like feathers brushing your skin. Or like blades of grass

when you pull them backwards between your fingers," I replied. The spider was now at my jawline, reaching her arms up over the ridge there toward my lips. I felt her gentle hands on my mouth, my upper lip, touching inquisitively on the edge of my nose. Her body moved across my face, the prickly hairs of her abdomen sliding across my upper cheek. I tilted my face to offer her a flatter platform. Then, she marched over my eye, onto my forehead, and stopped on the top of my head, Everest conquered.

At the boy's suggestion, I offered her my palm and she climbed aboard. I no longer turned my face away from her. In fact, I could not take my eyes off her. When I stroked her back with the top of my finger, she seemed to rise to the touch. Far, far too soon, the time came to return her to her tank. When I left the pet shop that afternoon, I felt as though I were betraying her by leaving her there.

The spider and I had accomplished a miracle together that afternoon. I brought myself, my fear, and my willingness for things to be different to that pet shop, and the spider brought me the transformative mystery of herself. Across the barriers of culture and species, she spoke to me of life as it looks encased in a stiff and fragile body. From inside of that body — a small and hairy thing — she revealed to me simply and masterfully that a larger body of mind and spirit resided there. I don't know what, if anything, I revealed to her. I hope in some way she felt through my skin a sense of my awe and appreciation of her, and of my unspeakable gratitude toward her.

I never saw spiders with the same eyes after that day. When I moved into my first rental trailer several years later and found it already inhabited by hoards of black house spiders, I was able to modify my spider vocabulary from "invaders" to "roommates" and find a way to live in peace with them, asking only that they not fall from the ceiling onto my face in the middle of the night. None did.

Just this past year, while cleaning my bedroom, I came across a small jumping spider moving across the surface of my sliding patio door. Thirty-four years have passed since my encounter with the tarantula. In the ensuing years, I have escorted many spiders outside in cups and on tissues. Many more I have simply let share the sink, the corners, the ceilings. Jumping spiders have become a special love of mine, with their flying, saucer-shaped bodies and rows of portal-like black eyes. This one was so small, a tiny animated jewel no bigger than a piece of cracked corn.

I needed to clean the glass doors, so the spider had to go somewhere else. On a whim, I spoke to her, saying, "If you climb onto my finger tip, I'll take you to a better, safer place than this." Always before, when I extended my digits to spiders, they recoiled and ran. But this day was different. The jumping spider stood her ground as my index finger touched down like a mountain in front of her. After maybe five full seconds of quiet deliberation, she reached out a leg as fine as an eyelash and touched my finger, probing as far as she could reach. Satisfied, she gathered her legs beneath her and launched herself onto my fingernail. Never once did she move while I carried her slowly to the spider plant in the bathroom. When I said, "This is the place," she launched again onto a leaf and scurried away into the plant forest. A person, I thought. A spider-person of great courage and trust.

For decades after my face-to-face meeting with the tarantula — my ultimate spider — I would read about the mythol-
ogy of the Spider, and about Spider as creator of the first
alphabet. I believe now that Spider was calling me to my true
work as a writer, and that my fear of Spider was wedded in
part to my fears of claiming my dormant skills as a weaver of
alphabets.

When I recall my tarantula experience, which I often do,
what remains vivid in my mind is not the color of her, or the
face of the clerk, or the particulars of the shop or the day.
The enduring clarity of sight and sensation attending those
memories rests solely in the numinousness of the encounter,
in the spiritual, almost holy sensation of meeting a deep fear
eye-to-eye and having the fear burst softly like an iridescent
soap bubble over your face. No one, myself included, could
have talked me out of my spider terrors. Instead, Spider herself, wordlessly and in the simple language of her own personhood, reached out and met me finger to finger, changing
my world forever in less time than it had ever taken my
mother to quell my fear with the swat of a well-aimed towel.

I think back to the small brown and pearl-colored spider
stepping gently across my covers who had made the innocent
and fatal error of coming to meet me when my fear was
uncontrollable and deadly. In my dreams, I choose to imagine
that she came back to Earth larger than life, with black bris-
tling hairs and pumpkin-colored stripes around her legs, and
that we met again, not simply face to face, but soul to soul.

Strange Relations

REPULSION, ROMANCE, AND BEFRIENDING

You should try to hear the name the Holy One has for things,
We name everything according to the number of legs it has;
The other one names things according to what they have inside.

— Jelalludin Rumi, "The Gift"

Although I wrote my story about Spider a long time ago, this is the one story that has not yet been sent off to my editor because I have not been able to craft the reflection piece to accompany it. I have struggled with this one for months, trusting somehow that the Grandmother of all spiders would come to me and let me know what to say. But as the days pass, Spider just sits and sits. And so I sit here, four days from my publishing deadline, asking again: "Please, Spider, tell me what to say."

Yet at the same time I am very vigorously ignoring what I am hearing because I do not want to write about it. Spider says, "Write about those emotions that are so strong they grab you and color your world for better and worse. Write about revulsion, yes, but write also about love — the kind of love that is as blind as fear. Write about bugs and romance because it is all of one fabric." My mind fogs, then blunders into a maze. What are the strands that can possibly connect insects and romance? Few would imagine the two linked in any way, shape, or form, save by someone on some pretty powerful hallucinogens. But I sense the beginning of a web-strand reverberating with a soft plink. I sit with my fingers poised over my keyboard.

Ah, there it is. Perhaps weaving together love and bugs is not really such an odd thing at all. Insects and romance both elicit strong, nearly uncontrollable emotions in many people. Anytime strong emotions sail onto our horizon, we are in sight of a huge opportunity to expand that horizon of Self in a powerful way. The opportunity for growth in these cases is large because the challenge is large: It is not easy to weather a turbulent emotional storm and keep your boat upright.

There is something powerful in juxtaposing perceived opposites like love and bugs. In our war on bugs, inflamed by our cultural revulsion to some of them (think of roaches, lice, maggots), we might expect to see our smallest, most guarded, most uncompassionate selves take charge. In the fire of romantic love (think of passion, adoration, infatuation), we may expect to encounter our most expansive, generous, and unguarded selves. My experience is that our expectations about anything are seldom correct, and this holds true for bugs and love.

I believe there are other likenesses between bugs and the lovebug: Both remain mysterious and strange at their core because we see them as so "not us." The ones who ignite passion in our hearts and bodies are certainly not us, we tell ourselves. If we believed they were us, we would not always be seeking the rush of enchanted love outside of ourselves. That perceived — and false — sense of extreme otherness is what makes our beloved so compelling and occasionally, because of the hugeness of the emotions, so repellent. In a similar way, we tell ourselves that the velvet bumblebee with the mysterious, gravity-defying body is not us, and so he retains his stunning, alluring mystery until he lands like a small buzzing prop plane on our arm and we shriek suddenly and swat him off. Mystery in both its most repellent and most attractive forms has much to reveal to us.

It seems worth remembering that romance and bugs can both sting. It also seems to me that we are about as limited in our capacity to offer friendship to bugs as we are to offer it to those we are in a passion over. I'll say more about this later.

Sitting beside my desk is Joanne Lauck's beautiful and unflinching study of the human-insect relationship. Her book, *The Voice of the Infinite in the Small,* came to me many years ago and has remained a reference for me not only about humans and bugs, but about humans and anything we feel the need to push away from ourselves. Joanne believes that it is not really the oddness of bugs that has us at war with them, but rather our cultural conditioning about them and the lack of context. Surely, my encounter with Spider speaks to that. But my invitation to the tarantula, while so brave at the time, seems a bit of a cakewalk in comparison to the invitations I find myself needing to extend not just to the six- or eight-leggeds around me, but to some of the two-leggeds as well.

Let me tell you a story. I will put it into the necessary web of words, but Spider weaves her silk through every inch of it. Some time ago, I was struck with Eros's arrow. That is, sparks flew from me to a fellow. It had been quite some time since this had happened to me. The last time, I was faltering on the edge of clinical depression, and my medicine bag for working with this kind of magic — and romance is surely the most powerful sort of magic — was depleted. Not so this time. My energy was strong, and, providentially, my resolution for the year had been to explore and extend love.

I had been asking love in many forms to seek me out. When she came to me in one of her most intoxicating guises, I was delighted that she arrived when my head was clear and my heart was full and joyful. However, the fellow I was suddenly aiming all this energy at was polite about his decision to remain out of any romantic fantasy. He was eager to pursue friendship, though, so we did.

I didn't know him well or long enough at that time to be disappointed much by the fact that my sparks were not going to be commingling with his. Instead, this one-way slice of romance opened the door for me to walk this enchanted path as an exploration of and by myself. It felt like a huge gift, and it really was just that. But you know, sometimes even the best medicine does not go down easily. It was a bit that way for me.

Spider meanders deliberately across my screen. She is towing something. It is a tiny sac of words — Joanne's words about insects. Spider drops them here and waits as I feel sweat forming on my palms: "The context sets the stage and determines whether we enter a battlefield, an amusement park, or a temple when we meet."[1]

Whether it's bugs or love, we often make assumptions about the stage on which we will meet. When it comes to insects, we nearly always expect to meet on battlefields, at least in our culture. We are lifelong soldiers when it comes to bugs. Yet I met my tarantula in a temple, just on the edge of a battlefield. I had expected the battlefield, but I had planned for it so well and deliberately that the grounds were miraculously transformed into an altar. I had prepared myself; I was open to relationship with the spider. If I had not readied myself, I never would have made it through the shop door.

In contrast, I met my friend in a romantic temple of my own making and design, and I came in with expectations that our transactions would always remain on temple grounds. I had done no preparation because our cultural history around romance tells us that we are fitted to this task and that love — unlike war — takes no preparation. Humans just *do* this. My social upbringing has taught me that I should expect to meet bugs on battlefields and that I should expect to meet passion in a temple. Culturally, the contexts are set in concrete and have been for many generations, if not for eons. Thus, I brought to my tarantula encounter more awareness than I did to my romantic one. We don't expect to find love with bugs, and we don't expect to find bugs in our love. In both cases, we cheat ourselves.

Spider spins her web across my screen and strums her strands at me, impatiently. "Get on with the story." Okay. As time passed my friendship with this fellow continued, and I nurtured my little slice of romance on the side. I watched it, spoke to it, wrote about it, mused over it, and fed it. I know how to do friendship, but this tiny slice of fire seized my attention because I had never entered this place in myself as a mature adult. And I so wanted to do it, now.

Confoundingly, I found that I was trying to have grown-up conversations with a giggling cherub who I now believe might have had eight legs. She was so unknown to me, strange-bodied and segmented, and my misconceptions about her left me open to stings. Yet those stings were much like venom — a toxin that can also be made into a medicine. Intentionally, I took hold of the energy of romantic love, and with prayer, ceremony, journaling, reflection, and dedicated self-will, I channeled it purposefully away from my friend and into every other area of my life, where it took seed and sprouted. My work life was recharged. My friendships deepened. My relationship with God became closer and more immediate. I was working hard, in earnest, and with 98 percent of my intention in complete alignment with my goal to dance in awareness with the cherub. I accomplished more growth than I would have ever thought possible.

And yet, there were days in my friendship with this man when I felt confused, awkward, stupid. This pain was not associated with our friendship. It was hidden in that tiny 2 percent of self-indulgent romance I still toyed with and would not give up because it was tasty and fun — like a glass of the sweetest wine that two-steps across your taste buds and twirls your mind. Just as in my dance with Spider a long time ago, no amount of thinking or analyzing could make contact with my feelings about this. In truth, that tiny, projected slice of infatuation was as powerful as heroin. As with Spider, it would take a face-to-face encounter with my friend to come to terms with it. And it would take me coming into the encounter prepared and awake, as I had come to the tarantula. But I did not know this then.

I need to digress here for one very important aside. This story illustrates in great part why stories and experiences put to paper are invaluable to me: They have an enigmatic way of producing so much more than my conscious mind could ever hope to bring to the table. This is why I write, and how I know that writing can heal. A tarantula has stepped forward from my history into my life today, and she has brought with her the gift of meaning and context. Stories can do this. And writing can deepen this process a hundred-fold.

Now I'll continue. The fellow and I met casually at a weekend workshop. Our last encounter, not long before, had involved an intense week of work together on an important project, the emotions of which were still powerfully with each of us. He entered the room, and I heard his voice behind me, talking to someone. And in that simple and shocking moment, I knew that he was suddenly not my friend. Not right then. Because if he were my friend, I would have easily known what to do and say. But I didn't know what to do. I stood frozen. There was this context, you see — two very separate contexts — and they were colliding to form a mass of stickiness, not a symmetrical, orb-shaped web but one of those dense mats of tangled silk strung in a dusty, forgotten corner. Would I meet him at a temple or on a battleground?

It is only in the writing of these words, right now, that I understand that I was trying to hold myself in two opposing contexts with this fellow. And I remember, in this moment, similar feelings with yet another friend. To this day, in the brief instances when romance melts into my friendship with him, I become momentarily awkward and self-conscious. I don't know what to do with my hands and my body. They become clumsy and don't fit well.

I stood to the side of the meeting room, feeling my muscles tense. This was my friend. Yet he was also the sweet wine I had been sipping ever so slowly. I felt the two separate contexts as if held in each hand, each one its own stone, each one bearing its own weight, its own desires.

Psychologist Robert Johnson, whose books I have read forward and backward, writes: "Romantic love...this curious blend of the numinous and the deadly...is not love that is directed at another human being; the passion of romance is always directed at our own projections, our own expectations, our own fantasies. In a very real sense, it is not a love of another person, but of ourselves."[2]

So could I, as a friend, meet this man in the temple, or would the tiny droplet of unmet desire that I carried for him sidestep me onto a battleground? Johnson cautions: "In romantic love, there is no friendship. Romance and friendship are utterly opposed energies, natural enemies with completely opposing motives.... When two people are 'in love,' people commonly say they are 'more than friends.' But in the long run, they seem to treat each other as less than friends."

I stood there with my back to him for only a split second, but it was time enough for me to hear volumes spoken from my heart. "Choose. You have a choice." I had chosen more easily with a tarantula, and yet that meeting and this one had a common foundation: This time, as with the Mother of All Spiders, I stepped forward with some preparation. The work I had done in fierce and deliberate earnestness to dance with the insect-bodied cherub — all the prayers, reflective walks, writings, ceremonies — came forward with me.

My friend approached me with a smile and a hug. I looked up to see the expression on his face. Suddenly, I realized he was standing between worlds, too — not the same worlds I stood between, but nonetheless, some inner landscapes of his own. The smile left his eyes and was replaced by the tiniest wisp of sadness.

In a fraction of a second, I looked my friend fully in the face and saw him with eyes similar to those I had turned on my precious tarantula. As she had stepped up onto my wrist, the contact with her and the simple sight of her had suddenly melted away my long history of cultural staining, terror, and consuming emotion because there was something even bigger than all that in the sheer presence of her. It was her sacred personhood. In the eyes of this man, I willed myself to see beyond my slice of enchantment and into the sacred personhood of him.

That sacred personhood of the Other has the power to heal all wounds between us and all our relations — two-leggeds and all the rest — because when the sacred is seen, it invites a precious third party to the encounter. Suddenly we are not left to mend our wounds alone. I am reminded of the twelve-step programs in which the addict admits to her helplessness and asks for help from a higher power. When we stand face to face with another being who intoxicates us with strong emotions that range from passion to repulsion to anger to fear, calling forth the sacred and putting it on the face of that Other is what can heal us and heal the world.

In the middle of the room at that workshop, I reached inside to find the piece of myself that is my friendship with this man. I would not meet my friend on a battleground, nor could I meet him in a temple. I was alone in that temple, anyhow. And so I did my best to meet him in a meadow, a place of friendship. What I accomplished in those brief moments between us was not complete, nor fully realized, just as my encounter with the tarantula was but a beginning in the transformation of my spider fears. But as with the tarantula, the moments of connection with him were genuine, open, and honest. They eventually lead me to a much deeper inquiry into certain misplaced parts of my ecstatic, romantic self. I cannot say on what ground my friend met me in those moments, any more than I can know where the tarantula met me. And it does not matter. Our work is uniquely our own.

On the final day of the workshop, we were asked to take a guided meditation in which we met ourselves at a time in our early lives before we were "wounded" in any way. I met myself in a flower-blanketed meadow. I was only three years old, and my hair was still the color of pale straw. I followed this child and at the same time was this child, and so when a large bumblebee landed on her fist, I could feel the upsurge of undiluted joy that coursed through her tiny, chubby-legged body. She fairly shook with delight and awe. In a tiny voice, she said to the insect, "Will you be my friend?" Bee-friend. I returned from the journey in tears, shaken at the mystery of synchronicity.

As I write these words, a gray spider about the size of a pea has come to sit on the edge of a drawing that hangs over my writing desk. She has long front legs and a very flat body. We have spiders in my neck of the woods that are poisonous. I never remember what they look like. So I look at this little flat girl and wonder if she is one of them, and I laugh at myself. She has brought me full circle, from repulsion, to romance, to the balm of befriending. Surely, whatever poison she might carry is medicine.

A Practice

Joanne Lauck suggests that the creatures and situations in our lives that are most frightening or repellent to us are actually extending us a powerful invitation to learn and to grow. So for this exercise, I would like you to find some living thing that is unattractive to you — not dangerous, just unattractive. It may be a particular insect, a weed that annoys you, an animal or a person you don't like. If you can arrange a face-to-face meeting with this being, all the better. If you need to do this in a meditation, it can still work, but the experience will be far less intense. With all the care and awareness you can bring into this moment, see if you can transform the ground upon which you meet this being from a battleground to a temple or a meadow. See what happens inside your feeling world as you prepare to make this shift to befriend the Other. Are you able to make this shift, easily or eventually? Whether you are successful or not, your emotions and feelings about this activity have much to teach you.

If you are unable to befriend this creature, try committing to this simple activity every day over a four-day period. Before each of your befriending sessions, repeat this portion of a quote from Carl Jung as a simple prayer: "On this day, God is the name by which I designate all things which cross my willful path." Let it be so.

C
H
A
P
T
E
R

N
I
N
E

Fashion

The dark bay thoroughbred mare who backed uncertainly from the rear of the too-small horse trailer was the tallest horse I'd ever seen. Her shoulders were like crested mountains and seemed to touch the clouds. Against the clear blue Wyoming sky, she was the color of deep wet soil. My hand brushed her neck as all four of her feet made contact with the earth again, and she shuddered beneath my touch and shifted sideways to get away from me.

Fashion was my first and only horse, given to me by my Native American friend and teacher, David Bearclaw. In native tradition, the gift of a horse is not to be taken lightly. It is a gift of great power, great honor. And so I was in no position to refuse the gift, although it came in a package I would have never, ever chosen myself. You see, my fantasy

horse was always short, tough, and willing — a mustang maybe, or a hardy mountain pony with legs like concrete pillars and a back as broad as a sofa. Fashion was certainly not short, tough, or on that particular July day, willing. She was an old, tall thoroughbred mare long off the racetrack, where she had once had a rare chance at greatness.

Standing beside her in the driveway, I could not help but notice that her right knee was thick with gnarled bone and arthritis, the result of a fracture that had taken her off the track and put her into early retirement more than fifteen years before. David had told me about it. She would be a good "first horse" for me, he had said. That knee would keep her from living her destiny as the swift, regal descendent of

the legendary Man O' War and prevent her from carrying
me on wild rides I was too green to handle.

From the lumpy burl on her knee, my eyes went next to
her feet. They were long and cracked, and she danced nerv-
ously in my driveway on clumpy, hurt toes like a ballerina in
wooden clogs. I could feel apprehension begin to rise up
lava-like from my ankles. Nervous diarrhea had splattered
the backs of her legs. She was thin. Her mane and tail were
a dusty mass of tangles, and her coat was dull. Corralled for
two years at the home of a man too frequently out of town,
she was a poster child for neglect — not abuse, mind you,
just neglect, like the neglect most of us have been guilty of at
one time or another, to one being or another. She had been
David's horse for many years, coming with him from the
horse farms in Kentucky, where he had been a top trainer. A
few years earlier he had given her to a friend, as a riding
horse for his wife. But the wife never rode her, and the man's
work took him away from home more and more.

Neglect settles down in a particularly harsh way on an
eighteen-year-old horse. Gone is the resilience of supple
bones, athletic flesh, firm skin. I felt it myself in my late, late
forties — that shocking and ominous loss of instant regener-
ation after a long day in the garden or a night or three of fitful sleep.

I stepped toward my gift horse and offered her my hand.
"Hello, Fashion. Welcome home." She turned her face away
and thrust her high head even higher into the air. Her breath
came in impatient snorts, and she scampered on the end of
her lead rope. I could have been a gnat, for all her interest in
me. David placed the lead rope into my hands. "Take the

lead. She's yours now." Trepidation mounting, I took hold of 16.2 hands of old, bony mare who had often stood covered with flowers in the winner's circle. "She could have been one of the great ones," David had told me, "if not for that knee." He looked at me and smiled broadly, nodding his head at the two of us as though he knew something that I didn't. With mixed emotions of gratitude and dread, I walked my gift horse up to the barn.

That night in bed, unable to sleep, I asked myself why this mare had come to me. What an utterly unlikely pair we made: me, a complete greenhorn, and she, a hot-blooded track horse with a bad knee and a distant attitude. What had David been thinking to give this horse to me? She'd kill me, I thought. If I didn't expire falling off her back, which was as high as a house, the vet bills to get her back on her feet would preclude me ever buying groceries again, and I'd starve to death.

I had yet another fear that I could not articulate at that time, a bigger fear that lurked far below my level of consciousness. I was afraid of her age. To me, her eighteen years signified the end of life — infirmity, crumbling — as much as my coming fiftieth year signified the same in my own life. My mother, past eighty, has a proverb she has been fond of since her mid-seventies: "Getting old is hell. Don't get old." A horsewoman friend says that most horses in our country do not live to be eighteen. Mostly it is because we do not let them. Old horses and old people are marginal and worthless in our culture, their "usefulness" to us as gone as their youth.

After a long night of fitful dreaming, I knew only two things for certain about Fashion and myself. First, I could not give her back. She was my gift horse, and that was that. Second, I trusted that she had been important to Dave, and I trusted Dave. His parting words to me were, "She is the best. That's all. You'll see." There was nothing to be done, then, but to care for her and to see where time would take us.

The sun was shining when I walked up to the barn that morning. Fashion stood like a dark tree rooted in the middle of the pasture, never looking my way until I stood in front of her with a halter and lead rope. And even then, all she offered was a passing glance that took me in and dismissed me, both in the same instant. She was easy to halter and to lead, and I tied her up to a fence post and began working the knots out of her mane and the dirt out of her coat while she gazed with blank expression at the mountains behind the house. Yet when I put a soft dust brush to her forehead, she came back into her body instantly, thrusting her head up and down against the length of the bristles over and over to get at every itch that ever was. I held the brush tightly in place, feeling the enormous power of her neck pushing against my hands. When she was done, she blew a blast of damp air from her nose and sighed heavily. Her eyes went back to the hills, and I once again felt as unnoticed as a barn fly flitting around her face.

What I wanted most from a horse was a relationship, a connection. The riding would have been a secondary thrill. I longed for Fashion to take notice of me, to like me instantly and completely, as my dogs had always liked me. But my Flicka fantasies faded as quickly as the waning summer days. She was not — how shall I say it? — effusive in her affections. She was not interested in the bonding that I sought. She had come to me after a long history that I could only imagine, and her personhood was set and secure. My own history — equally unknown to her — had carved me into a seeker of recognition. In all areas of my life, I seek to be known, to be seen. It has become my personal antidote for loneliness. And so I brought the needs of my own near half-century of living to the table with Fashion and was crestfallen that she was not interested in the intimacy and affirmation that I was trying to dish up between us.

For the rest of the summer, I resigned myself to being a caregiver. That was the relationship she allowed me. From July until October, I put money and time and energy into what horsey friends told me was a bottomless money hole — an older horse with a bum knee. Naturopathic vets, equine chiropractors and dentists, farriers, and horse-savvy neighbors trooped in and out of my barn, ran their hands over my gift horse's body and legs, peered into her mouth, and made their proclamations. I didn't know what advice to take and what to ignore, so I took it all. I drove Fashion all the way to Evanston, Wyoming, to meet a farrier who was touted as being the best of the best. He was. By the time he finished with Fashion's feet, the cracked clogs were gone and in their place were four fairy slippers. Her feet were tiny, lovely, and — the farrier snorted — hard as rocks. "Don't bother to shoe her. She has feet like rocks. Good horse you got here. Good horse, good feet."

My unlikely conglomeration of treatments, special supplements, exercises, and effort came together in a mysterious alchemical blending, and as the summer harvest ripened, Fashion began to look like the queen she must have once been. I spent hours brushing her and humming away in the shade of the barn, loving the rich, dusty smell of her and the heat of her skin against my hands. She had stopped her habit of moving away from the brushes, and sometimes I would see her faraway eyes slip into a contented doze, the lids like half-moons over the brown planets of her eyes. My favorite horse song was "Goodbye, old Paint, I'm leaving Cheyenne," and I sang it incessantly. By fall, I think even the barn wasps knew the words.

Fashion took on a shine, with big, golden dapples spread in a lush sheen over her liver-colored coat. Someone loaned me a very old saddle and a hackamore, and, overtaken by a total lack of good sense, I began to take Fashion out for short rides alone in the foothills beyond our house. One afternoon as we descended the hill behind my barn, she began leaping side to side in a burst of fall frolicking, and I jettisoned out of control off her back like a stone out of a slingshot. She stopped, stunned, and put her head down to sniff me. I don't imagine she had ever seen a rider become unglued so fast, and it was a revelation to both of us. In all our future rides, I somehow managed to stay aboard, but not like a rider, really — more like a determined tick.

I began to see why David believed that Fashion and I would be good for each other. Elder horses have a quality that is hard to put a name to, a certain sense of composure and acceptance that serves true greenhorns well. When we rode together, I always felt as though I were going on an outing with Everywoman's mythic grandma — the grandma who exudes comfort and wisdom and whose no-nonsense approach to the world abides no whining. With such a grandma, we are emotionally safe forever.

As any good grandmother will do, Fashion began the immense task of teaching me how to spend safe time in the company of others — in this case, horse others. I learned to watch her feet, because when I didn't she would step on me, then lean in and grind my foot into the sawdust. She showed me how easy it is to get your head bonked squeezing under a horse's chin to grab a manure rake. She showed me how quickly you can get squashed up against the side of a stall when you are not watching what you are doing. And she taught me that all hell can break loose around horses when you least expect it.

Miraculously, she taught all these lessons without hurting me. David told me she had been born self-assured and royally confident. So strong was her sense of self that my constant fumbling and lack of horse skills had no effect on her whatsoever. Fashion trusted herself in a way that was refreshing and thought provoking for me. In her presence, I wondered often what it must be like to live so comfortably in one's own skin, and I sensed that the ripening of age had some part in the process. While my mother told me that growing old is "the pits," Fashion told me something different, although at the time, I thought she was teaching me only about horses and riders.

In caring for my gift horse, I reconnected daily to the joy of giving simply for its own sake. Some animals you care for clearly appreciate what you do for them, but this was not the case with Fashion, for whom I was simply "the staff." In her eyes, I was put on Earth to care for horses, and she was generously enabling me to do that. But on one day late in the fall, when the mountain breezes were crisp and the sun was as yellow as lemons, my gift horse graced me with an unexpected, immense gift of her own. This gift made all my fussing and tending and care-taking pale in comparison.

It began simply enough on that sunny fall morning when I spotted Fashion lying in a heap in the west corner of the pasture. It was her favorite spot for sunning. Halter in hand, I headed her way in hopes of an early ride before the sun got too hot. Usually, Fashion would hurry to her feet the moment she sensed me coming, but this day she remained down, fairly groaning with the joy of the early sun on her side and face.

Caught up in the quiet bliss of the moment, I moved quietly to her head and knelt down beside her. "Want to go for a ride, pretty one?" She opened one liquid-brown eye and gazed into my face. Then her sleepy eye spotted the blue halter. With a heavy sigh she nosed the halter aside, and placed her enormous jug of a head on my lap. The eye closed, her rubbery lips twitched, and a soft snore rumbled from her chest. I stroked her soft cheeks and rubbed her leaf-like ears between my fingers. The solid weight of her head sank deep against my legs and stomach. I could feel the warmth of her face and the hardness of her jaw. She twitched her ears at the buzz of a fly, and her snoring deepened. The summer grass was old now, bent dry and yellow beneath us.

Time ran down and stopped, and we rested together in a moment that was complete and perfect. Emotions shivered through me as I pressed my palm to Fashion's face again and again, drinking up the rare, precious moment of feminine intimacy, friendship, and recognition. Finally, she had seen me, and the sweetness of her gift to me was like cool water after a four-day fast. It struck me so deeply that I would never forget it — this moment of being seen after trying so hard, almost desperately, to make myself visible.

When we at last rose to our feet — stiffly, as old girls do — we had changed. In those few, sacred moments, we had become the companions David must have been seeing in his mind's eye when he placed the lead rope of a gift horse into my uncertain and unknowing hands. I know the old saying "Never look a gift horse in the mouth" has to do with long teeth and aging and gratitude. But the saying is not quite right. Instead, it should be simply, "Never doubt a gift horse." Ever.

Unseen Relations

A PRAYER FOR SIGHT

"Peek-a-boo . . . I see you!"

— Baby game

My friend has seven horses. I am capable of riding only two of them, the two oldest: Brownie and Paint. Last week, my friend's daughter asked her, "Mom, what are you going to do with Paint when his arthritis is so bad you can't ride him anymore?" My friend said, "I don't have to think about that now."

But I am thinking about it now. I am thinking about how old horses and old people become quietly unseen simply by virtue of their age. And more important, I am thinking about what it means to be visible and invisible. I am in my fifties now, facing bodily changes accelerated by the radiation treatments I had sixteen years ago. At least I tell myself it was the radiation. Maybe this happens to most women in their fifties — the loss of mental clarity, of strength, of memory. As my hair grays, I, too, will start to become invisible to my culture.

I live with my mother, who is in her early eighties. If you told me three years ago that I would be living comfortably with my mother, I would have laughed, or maybe cried. For many years, I felt invisible to my mother, our closeness lost to me by the simple blistering of typical mother-daughter growing pains. In many ways, I felt dismissed by my mother because I was too young and too unlearned to understand that sometimes the dismissal we feel is commensurate with the dismissal we bestow on others. It feels as though it is aimed our way by another, but it is really quite often a boomerang sent off with our own hand. This dynamic is often part of the dance between children and their parents.

Feelings of invisibility and dismissal are known to all of us at one time or another, that heart-aching knowledge that we are unseen — that some important aspect of ourselves or some big fear that is real to us is invisible to and unacknowledged by another. So making someone *visible* is a profound dynamic, and we begin our dance with it early. There is a simple game, for instance, that we play with infants, in which the symbolism is anything but simple. Do you remember it? Have you ever stood over a cradle and hidden your face from a baby? Have you made your voice silly, and said, "Peek-a-boo! I see you!" and pulled your hands to the side, just in time to see that baby's face light up like a Christmas tree? Can you remember the giggling, the gasps, the happy surprise? My relatives played this game with me, and I have even played it with my dogs and cats. There is something of primordial importance to being seen. I don't know what it is, but I know it is necessary to life, in big and small ways.

My pure moment of awareness with Fashion in the autumn pasture is one of my most enduring touchstones for reflecting on the gift of seeing and being seen, but I need to begin my prayer for this particular kind of vision not with Fashion, or with babies, but with a story about my mother.

Let me begin by saying that my relationship with my

mother has been complex, filled with affection, contention, anger, posturing, control, and lessons — oh yes, endless lessons. I love my mother, and she makes me absolutely crazy. My mother is beautiful in a glorious sort of way, with a face wrinkled like a topography map and eyes that are a brilliant, near-startling blue. Age has shrunk her a few inches. She is blessed with white, white hair that she has worn in a bun since before it ever started turning color, half a lifetime ago. She still has more energy most days than I ever had or ever will have. When people first meet her they are frequently completely enchanted with her. "Your mother," they gush, "is just so...so...amazing!" I used to say this same thing to my friend Claire about her mother, to which she would respond, "Yes, she is, and she's not your mother. It's different when they are your mother, you know." Yes, I know.

I have spent much of my adult life living far away from my mother. Sometimes, in my tortured youth, this distance was by design. I would joke, "Five hundred miles is as close to home as I want to get." Like any animal seeking its own place in the world, I found that distance between us, and my need for it, served me. In *The Heroine's Journey,* family therapist Maureen Murdock writes: "The separation from the personal mother is a particularly intense process for a daughter because she has to separate from the one who is herself....Many daughters experience a conflict between wanting a freer life than their mother and wanting their mother's love and approval....Geographical separation may be the only way at first to resolve the tension between a daughter's need to grow up and her desire to please her mother."[1]

It took me a long, long time to "grow up," and so I left home, returned, and left again many, many times. Last winter, that changed. Last winter, I succumbed to an old cliché and "ran home to mother," and I have never left. Actually, I didn't run. I crawled, barely making it. She even had to help me get there.

Depression runs in our family, across generations and lineages. An uncle I never knew threw himself from a rooftop. It is said of a certain aunt that she died of a broken heart. My mother has battled clinical depression all of her life. Last year, I got to do my second dance with that dark sister, Melancholy. She had struck me once before, but never like she did last winter. Over the course of many months and through a series of health issues, combined with a challenging set of life circumstances, I got to the point where I literally could not drive without the road weaving in front of me, or feed myself unless it was canned food because even a frozen pizza seemed too complex a meal to tackle. Dust balls rolled through my house like tumbleweeds when vacuuming became an emotional event I was unfit to manage.

But when I started to like the isolating bubble I felt myself to be in, when I began to invoke it and rest quietly and unflinchingly in it, my counselor recommended a change of scene. If I had wanted, he would have signed the papers to commit me to the hospital for a voluntary three-month stay. Instead, I decided I would go to my mother's house and stay for the winter. Once I made that decision, which took weeks, I realized I was not capable of making the cross-country drive to get there. So a few days after New Year's my mother showed up with her sweetheart, Bill, and they bundled me up, along with the dogs, cat, and my computer, and drove me to the northwest coast of California, to her home in a grove of redwood trees.

We have a joke about my mom in our family. She is the queen of "Yes...but." To every suggestion you will ever make to her about anything, she will offer this extraordinarily exasperating phrase. Even when she needs help — no, *especially* when she needs help. It is frustrating beyond belief to watch every good piece of advice you give get flushed down the toilet of "Yes...but" while Mom gazes up at you with those blue and resolute eyes.

So imagine my utter shock when I got to the redwoods and began chirping "Yes...but" to everyone who came to visit me in my greatly debilitated state. The advice of my family and friends was gentle and well intended: "You should go walking on the beach...sit in the redwoods... bake bread...get out more...start writing again...go shopping...eat better..." It was all such good advice, and I could do none of it. Mostly, I spent my days in a stupor, watching it rain and sleeping late. It is not possible to explain depression to those who have never suffered from it. Even if it were, it was too exhausting to try. My short version of the story simply became "Yes...but." Those around me could grasp that it was too cold to walk, too much bother to bake bread, and too expensive to go shopping much more easily than they could understand that it was not possible for me to walk, to speak, to shop, or to perk up.

Hearing my mother in my own mouth, I began to understand over the weeks how much of Mom's personality had been built around protecting herself in her lifelong battle with clinical depression. She suffered melancholy in an era when such things were totally misunderstood. And Mom never had "the blues." She had "the blacks." That winter, I began to realize for the first time that what I had often perceived as my mother's emotional unavailability in my young years had nothing, nothing to do with me. Depression strips your ability to be emotionally available to anyone, self included. My gut sense as a toddler that Mom was sometimes not quite "there" was accurate, but her distance and her strategies for shielding it did not come from a lack of love for me, my brother, and my father. This realization was nothing short of a revelation to me, and it heralded the germination of a fundamental change in my relationship with her.

Medical intuitive Carolyn Myss advises that it is unhealthy to bond with others through your wounds, but as the winter progressed, it was the language of depression that put my mother and me on common ground for the first time in our lives, and it was healing. Over chicken soup, my mother would look at me with worry in her eyes and say, "I know how you feel." And for the first time in fifty-one years of living, I believed her.

Can you hear Fashion's breath over my shoulder as I write this? Can you hear how deeply I needed to be heard and seen by someone for healing to germinate in the frozen soil of my heart? That winter, Fashion was in the breath of my mother, simply holding the space for me to be seen, to see myself, so that I would not blow away.

By March, I had recuperated enough that I could begin to appreciate the importance of what I had been given over the winter. The gift to me had been no less than a deepening of compassion for myself and for all things that suffer. As the first azaleas began to bloom red and pink in the redwood stumps of Mom's yard, Fashion's memory came into the space between us yet again to deepen the learning.

I was heading for San Francisco with a friend for four days of unexpected work. As I slipped into the passenger seat of the car with my travel bag, Mom carried my purse to me. Our words to each other were tense. Her mouth was a hard line and her face carried a lost look that I believed she had cultivated just to aim at me. Because of my trip, Mom would need to change a dental appointment I had set up for her, as she does not drive — never has, never will. The broken appointment hung between us like poison gas. "How can I ever know that anything I really need will get done?" she murmured, distantly, as she handed my purse through the open window.

"It will. I'll be back soon," I said as I turned my face away and drove off with my friend. For the first miles of the drive, behind the lively conversation I was having, I was thinking about my mother: "You have no regular schedule. What do you care when things get done? I always get them done. Why are old people so annoying and bossy and stubborn?…"

Somewhere outside of Cloverdale, I suddenly felt the weight of Fashion's huge head in my lap. We all need to be seen. Wasn't that the gift my elderly horse gave to me? To just see me and acknowledge my existence? Is it that simple? Is that all my mother is asking? A memory of summer washed over me. A memory of myself standing not beside Fashion, but beside my friend's old horse, Paint.

Paint, a brown and white pinto, had come from difficult circumstances. He responded to the lack of affection and honor in his previous life by trusting no one. A steady, small, and persevering mount, Paint would carry anyone anywhere without complaint, but he would not let you thank him in any way. It was a thing of his, to refuse any offer of a carrot, a handful of grain, an apple. And so of course, I wanted nothing more in the world than to have him take something from my hand, to acknowledge in some way my gratitude for his carrying me over hill and dale and back again safely and surely.

I always took special care grooming him before my rides. I offered him small moments of massage around his legs and lips and ears, and whispered encouraging and grateful words to him all through our rides together. He was the perfect horse to sing "Goodbye, Old Paint" to, and as I did, he would flick his ears to the words and seem to enjoy it. On my last ride of the summer, I stood before him after pulling the saddle off his back. I had an apple in my hand. It was late in the day and the shadows were long. Insects crooned around us. My hand raised the apple to Paint's nose, and he reached forward to sniff it. His soft lips parted and he put his teeth to the apple skin, bit, and chewed. I stood as still as a post, my whole being scarcely daring to believe the moment.

Today, it is not the rides I most vividly remember about Paint, although we have been on a few grand ones. It is not the singing to him or the loping along a flat forest trail or his bouncing trot. It is that moment with his lips around the apple and me standing as still as stone with my jaw hanging open and the hair on my neck prickling. That was the best.

Being seen. My pasture moment with Fashion was the same: It was the best of all our moments together, the moment she saw me. Two old horses — arthritic, a bit sore, one as tall as a house, the other as tiny as a painted fairy — bringing me the sacred gift of recognition and acknowledgment.

Now I am back in the car near Cloverdale, feeling the weight of Fashion's head in my lap and the touch of Paint's nose on my wrist, remembering the longing eyes of my mother as she stood in the driveway, my purse extended to me in her hands. And for a moment, I know I am as Fashion and Paint, with my head high in the air and my eyes on a distant horizon. Will I see my mother? Will I see her as a being of consequence? My friend drives and the car sings along through the town, past stop lights and stores, and on the south side of its borders, the larger truth collides with me. What do I most want? To be seen. What does my mother want? To be seen. Why don't I see her? Because she has become invisible with age. Her needs seem silly to me, confrontational, blown all out of proportion.

Two old horses who live in my heart bow their heads my way. One has a face of coffee brown with a white half-star on her forehead. The other is spotted brown and white. Both have grown stiff and sore with life. Both are becoming invisible, as their age overshadows all that they are and have been. Many would now see them as only two sets of stiff legs, or two wallet-drainers. Age is not by any means the whole or even the half of it. Paint and Fashion are ambassadors for the many, many others who by virtue of our fears, our perceptions, our values are unseen in our culture. Children are often invisible. Homeless people always are. Animals are seldom seen for all that they are. The Earth herself is invisible to many of us.

And yet these two old horses saw me, in moments when I needed to be seen as more than a caretaker, more than a blob to be carried upright in a saddle. Two old horses gave me a visceral sense of what it means to be dismissed, and what it feels like in glorious and healing moments to be seen. Each saw me in moments that were so huge for me I could never forget them.

To be seen restores the heart of the one suddenly visible. It brings a moment of peace, of comfort, of safety, of grace. I know this because of the joy of moments when I have been seen, and from the pain of moments when I have not. When I returned from my trip to San Francisco, I told my mother I would make her needs a priority, and that she could trust that. She was appreciative, but she reminds me to this day that my ill-timed trip is the reason her lower dentures have never fit right. Still, I think I have done a fair job now of making certain my mother feels visible.

Extending this concept beyond my mother, I have been much more aware of the need to make visible all of life around me. Sometimes this seeing and acknowledging is inconvenient — to say the least. It means I have to slow down, to listen, to change my schedule, to quiet my own internal voices that want to be heard first and always. But I have memories that sustain me in this new prayer of making all beings visible: The feel of a solid equine head in my lap, the touch of old horse teeth against a green apple.

And I have a memory of last winter when my mother saw me, too, because I let her see me. I allowed her to nourish me with a certain look in her blue eyes and a bowl of chicken soup in her hands. Becoming visible to my mother restored a piece of my life to me. Taking the time to truly see her after my return from San Francisco restored a part of hers. We each have another Mother — common to all of us — who is literally dying to be seen. My prayer is that we can make her visible and in doing so, restore life to the Earth and to ourselves.

A Practice

Go outside and find a piece of your mother — your Earth Mother. She may be resting in a corner of your yard or patio, or sending small, determined green shoots up from a crack in the pavement. If you are blessed she will be close by, in trees, in a small park, an empty, wild lot, a lake or stream. Do not hurry. Take every distracting thought about where you need to really be and what you think you really ought to be doing, and mentally wrap those thoughts in a piece of red cloth, tie it with a string, and set it down next to you. It will be there for you to pick up when you are done, if you really want to.

Close your eyes and breathe fully and deeply. When you open your eyes, do so with the intention to see, to receive this place. With open eyes, see with your heart and with your emotional body, as well as with your eyes. Receive whatever gifts this small piece of your Great Mother has for you. You might feel delighted, elated, saddened, or raw. It is all a gift of your willingness to see, and it is all perfect.

When you feel complete, close your eyes again. Breathe.

When you open your eyes once more, do so with the intention of being seen. For a moment, allow this Mother to fully see and receive you. There is never a moment when she does not, but it is easy to forget this. Letting your experience with visibility spill out on the page of your journal will make this process more powerful than you can imagine.

Kulu

I remember looking at his ears and thinking, "The parts that are bitten off will not grow back." Still, perhaps I expected they would. We looked at each other that summer day from across a distance that seemed like lifetimes, but it was only a moat that separated us. Only a narrow band of shallow, popcorn-dirtied water that protected the chimps on the island from us, and us from them. The tiled floor space of Chimp Island held two baby chimps that day. One of them was a bread box–sized, delicate-looking female with slender fingers and huge eyes. The other one was Kulu.

What can I say about Kulu? I will say, to start, that he was my son, or as close to one as I will have in this lifetime.

I first met him when I was practically a child myself — a tender, immature nineteen years to his innocent thirteen months. I lived with Mom and Dad still, and thanks to my mother's networking, I had landed a coveted job at a local "baby zoo." I loved this job, and from the moment I took it I didn't for a minute think that life could get any better, until the zoo's owner asked me one Saturday if I would like to be the primary keeper for the baby chimpanzee he had just purchased from another zoo.

Don't think that I was selected because I was somehow more gifted with animals than the rest of the workers. No, the honest truth was that I was chosen because I had more spare time. And Kulu, the baby chimpanzee, would need considerable home care before he was able to spend full days and nights all by himself at the zoo. Kulu would need to spend time with me and my family for a while, getting his "zoo legs" under him. Perhaps I was also selected in small part because of the unexpected success I'd had several weeks before with an orphan pygmy goat who had been given up for dead.

All I knew the day my girlfriend Debbie and I excitedly piled into her Toyota for our long, hot ride to the zoo was that we would be bringing back to my house a young chimpanzee who was to sleep at night in a large cage in our daylight basement, and to spend the rest of the time "getting adjusted" to me. That I had never so much as held a baby chimpanzee in my life did not faze me in the least. I was so bold and self-assured at nineteen that I didn't even bother to read Jane Goodall's books in preparation for my primate motherhood. All I knew was that the miles could not race by fast enough, and we drove much of the way to that zoo at speeds in excess of ninety miles an hour.

When we finally arrived, Debbie and I were led to the zoo's infant quarters. While the staff scurried around to locate an appropriate carrying cage for our expensive cargo, I was introduced to the woman who had been Kulu's caretaker since he had been taken from his own mother only a few days after he was born. In those days, it was common practice in many zoos to take chimpanzee infants from their mothers. The mortality rate was lower when the babies were raised by humans, I was told. Kulu's keeper was a young woman, much like me but with a sense of softness and introspection that I hadn't yet developed. She showed me a book of photos of Kulu as a tiny baby the size of a soda can, and she spoke of him in words that seemed measured and carefully selected.

"Can I see him?" I interrupted.

"Not quite yet. Um...let me tell you some things about Kulu..." She spoke quietly and took a moment to look full into my eyes before she continued. "What do you know about baby chimps?" she asked. When I admitted I knew just about nothing, she said, "Okay, we'll go from the beginning...

"When a baby chimp is taken from its mother, it needs to bond with its keeper, to recognize that keeper as Mother, in order for it to thrive. Kulu — it's Swahili for 'little boy' — was taken when he was very young. It was very traumatic for all of us. His mother fought and there was a lot of commotion and upset. I don't know if that had anything to do with it, but the truth is," she let out a breath and brushed her brunette hair away from her eyes, "the truth is, for some reason, Kulu never accepted me as his mother. I can handle him, and he is polite and resigned to it, but we never bonded. I wanted to, and he didn't. Sometimes it happens that way. It has been...hard for us. Hard for him. He is a little ...difficult to handle sometimes. He's afraid. Do you understand what I'm saying?"

Blessedly, I hadn't a clue what she was saying. I did not know that even at Kulu's tender age, he could bite hard enough to leave scars, and that his fingers were strong enough to dig into flesh and leave blood and bruises if he wanted to. In my delirious, joyful oblivion, I just wanted the talking to be over and Kulu to be in Debbie's car. A steel cage with a solid door was put on a table near my purse. "Can't I just carry him in my arms?" I asked. The group around me shared looks, and someone said, "Probably not. We'll get him loaded for you and get his files together for you to take back."

On a whim I asked, "Could you please let me see him and sit with him in his room before you load him?" I sensed that it might be good for him to at least be able to recognize me as someone he had seen on his own turf before he was put into the carrying cage. It was the best call I could have made.

"Yes," said his keeper, "He's in here."

I see it still — the aviary-like room with a small floor and towering, glass-paned walls, the dead tree snaking long limbs high up from the floor. Sitting at the bottom of the tree with his arms wrapped around the trunk was Kulu, a small, white-faced chimpanzee about the size of a human baby. He backed up when I entered, turned away from the monkey biscuit I offered, and walked away from me upright on wobbly legs, arms held out for balance. "Just like a baby," I thought, "He moves just like a human baby." He dismissed me, not looking at me except to glance at me sideways to be sure I was not going to try and grab him. He kept beyond arm's length and kept his eyes blank and unreadable. Even in his infancy, there was a dignity to him that made me feel entirely out of my element. I felt awkward, self-conscious, and clumsy. At thirteen months, he had far more presence than I did. He always would.

I sat quietly with him, trying to beam him my good intentions. He would have none of it. I left the enclosure, and two of his keepers stepped in. They told me to leave. Debbie and I picked up our purses and coats and stepped into the office outside. The screaming began as soon as I shut the office door, a deafening shriek that would not let up. One of the keepers shouted out instructions on Kulu's care and feeding habits while handing me documentation of the sale. I shouted back a question about whether Kulu knew about diapers or not. My boss had told me we would need to get him in diapers quickly. "Yes," the young man yelled back, "When you approach him with a diaper, he thinks you are going to kill him, and he'll try to bite you. Be careful. He bites really hard."

The door opened and the noise became unbearable. Kulu's screams echoed from the steel box, and we carried the cage to the car with our free hands held over our ears. In the car, the screaming continued. Chimps can scream for hours. They have enormously strong lungs. The keepers shouted goodbye. Kulu's caretaker leaned over and put her lips to my ear and spoke to me in a volume reserved for dance floors when loud music is blaring. "I pray he'll let you be a mother to him. I pray it." We rolled up the windows and drove off in an ear-splitting cloud of noise.

It didn't last too long. At the sound and motion of the car engine, Kulu began to wind down, and his screams turned into muffled whimpers and cries. Then, in rhythm with the sound of the engine, he began a ceaseless, mono-tone moaning. It was a terrible, piteous sound, one that could crack a stone heart in two. Debbie and I looked at each other and said nothing as we sped out of town as fast as we could drive. What had life meant to him so far? How many

losses had he already suffered? How deeply did he suffer?
Did he have any sense of hope? Do any animals feel hope?

Finally, the noise stopped altogether, and we heard nothing from Kulu for the rest of the drive. By the time we
reached my house late in the afternoon, the whole neighborhood had turned out for "the monkey." I told the neighbors
that Kulu was too traumatized to visit, and Mom escorted a
large bunch of disappointed people down the driveway.
Debbie left, and with my father's help I carried Kulu's cage
into our small house and into an even smaller hallway that I
could close off at both ends. I remember being in a bit of a
daze from the long drive but just as impatient and eager to
get a glimpse of the chimp as the neighbors had been. I
opened the cage immediately, armed with a large beach towel
in case Kulu should charge out at me, screaming and flailing.
Of course, there was none of that. There was not a sound,
not a movement. Using a flashlight to see into the cage, I saw
him curled up in a shaking, miserable black ball as far away
from the door as he could get. Making my voice soft and
inviting did not help. Reaching for him gently did not help,
and he lunged at me fiercely with a loud hoot and pounded
his fists on the floor of the cage before scuttling back into his
dark corner. Then, he cried. Just like a baby.

I waited a long, long time. We left him alone, going into the hall now and again to check on him. He would not
leave the cage. Finally, in a desperate move, I reached inside
with the towel wrapped around my hands and pried him
out. I could not believe his strength. He hung onto the back
wall like a tick. Plaintive weeping was instantly transformed
into that now-familiar cacophonous, flailing screech. I had

one brief look at his face — contorted into a mass of wrinkles, grimacing white teeth, and round, shocked eyes — before instinctively pulling him tight against my chest and wrapping my arms around him.

"Oh, poor, poor sweet baby…" I cooed. "Sweet baby Kulu. My sweet boy…" I kissed the top of his head, all sticky with sweat and urine. Immediately, the screaming dropped away and was replaced by a soft, mournful hooting sound: "Ooooh…oooooh…hooooooh." He clutched at my clothes and buried his face in my sweatshirt, his damp body shaking with sobs. "Ooooh…" he cried, "Oooooh hooooh hooooh."

I stood there in the hallway, listening as the dark wooden floors magnified the hollow echo of his sad calls. In the dim light, my shadow fell over him. I stroked his head and tried to turn his face up to me, but he jerked away in fear and flattened his face against my chest. It suddenly occurred to me that it might be nearly impossible to pry his body off me. First, I couldn't get near him, then I couldn't get away from him. For the next hour, attempts on my part to put air space between us resulted in instant screaming. So I carried him from room to room, holding him against me at the table where Mom set out soup and rolls for dinner. After the meal, I sat on the sofa and read for a bit while his breath and his drool dampened my sweatshirt. My decision to visit him in his aviary before we moved was providential. I knew that I was now the only fragile shred of familiarity in a world gone catastrophic for him.

Chimpanzees' arms are as strong as their lungs. Kulu never lessened his grip on me that night, and I could not bear the trauma of trying to break him free. So I went to bed fully dressed and held him under the covers with me, where he clung tight all night.

I cannot tell you Kulu's story without also telling you something of zoos, of my experience of them anyway. I make no apology for my subjectivity. I have reflected on what I learned from Kulu and from that zoo for many, many years. They were sobering lessons.

In the beginning of my days with Kulu, I learned that while his physical health was of prime importance to the zoo owners, his emotional and spiritual health were not. The day after Kulu came to my home, I was told that he would be the zoo "guest" on the children's TV show *Romper Room* that week. Stunned, I advised my boss that the quaking bundle of anxieties that was Kulu was in no way ready for a public appearance. I knew that the owners understood exactly why they had gotten Kulu for a bargain price. They knew of his behaviors, his trauma. But no matter. Our *Romper Room* visit had been scheduled. I had only three days to prepare him for diapers, rides in cars, curious kids, handling by complete strangers, and camera lights. We had to start work immediately. Kulu would not have even one full day to rest up, to adjust, to grieve.

I was angry with my bosses, up to my eyeballs with righteous indignation. Although I had not yet acknowledged it — gads, there was no time to acknowledge anything! — something had happened to me when Kulu plastered himself to my body the night before. Regardless of how he felt about me, I was hopelessly, devotedly, eternally his. In a span of hours, I came to feel that Kulu had been with me forever. My maternal protectiveness kicked in immediately. I don't know if this sudden, intense bonding was a result of the calamitous horror of the day before, with all its noise and sadness, but when Kulu finally raised his eyes and looked up at me from his cave beneath my quilt in the quiet of late night, his face was full of babylove. We had both been transformed. I caught my breath as he touched my nose with his boney finger, then stuck the digit inquisitively but gently up my nose, murmuring a soft "Ooooh…" I sneezed, smitten to the bone.

God bless my mother, and God bless the inborn courage of incarcerated baby animals who turn their emotional lives inside out for us because they have no choice. We approached the diaper thing first, and with great dread, on the morning of Kulu's first full day with us.

With my mom dangling a banana and a cat toy in front of his nose, Kulu eventually allowed me to slip a diaper around his legs and fasten it with pins. When I was finished, he stood up and looked at this strange white blob stuck around his behind and fingered the pins with delicate wonder. He looked up at Mom and me and asked a quizzical "Oooh?" We clapped our hands and made a great, great fuss over him, and he never, ever tried to pull the diaper off. Not even once.

That evening, I reclined on the sofa with Kulu, in his new diaper and baby tee shirt, and pretended I was sorting through the hairs on his head for lice as he scrutinized and picked through every hair on my arm. He began smiling in earnest that first night, his grin as open and bright as the sun. Exploring my teeth was a source of special delight to him. I let him pull down my lips and tap at my teeth. Then, he pulled open my jaw and peered curiously into my mouth.

"Oooh," he exclaimed, as a child might say, "Oh, my!" In turn, he allowed me to finger his ears and stroke his lips, and to inspect his hands and fingernails.

Chimps have, to our sensibilities, rather ghoulish hands. They are like ours, but not like ours. We are used to fat baby hands, all pink and plump. But a chimp's hands always look as old as the ages: lined, weathered, blotchy. Kulu's nails were black and dull, and no matter how clean his hands were, they always looked a bit grubby. Still, for all their hairy untidiness, his hands were soft and incredibly dexterous, and far more under his control than are an infant's clumsy paws. As he held onto my lip with one hand and explored along my molars with the other, I thought that he might make a skilled surgeon.

On our second night together, I was told by my bosses that I must get him sleeping in his night cage, to prepare him for the lonely nights to come at the zoo. In the wild, a chimp would never sleep away from his mother. Such separation would feel like death and could easily result in death. But the fact that my son would be stressed or what such unnatural demands might do to his soul were of little concern to my bosses. So that night, I pulled off Kulu's diaper, filled his cage with banana slices, and coaxed him to exchange his hold on me for a bite of fruit. I betrayed him well, and when I closed the door behind him and locked it, his screams cut me to the bone.

Remembering him there in his hay-filled night chambers alone and crying to himself is a memory that has cast an enormous shadow on my perception of animals in captivity. If you could have seen him, sitting with his head hanging, wringing his small hands in his lap, emitting those mournful sobs, you might see the world differently, too. When I try to imagine our stations changed, with me in that cage, abandoned, unsettled, the world around me utterly unfathomable, it feels like hell, like madness. I would ask myself, "What have I done? Why is this happening? Why?"

When the *Romper Room* date arrived, I knew Kulu was nowhere near ready for the event. Although he had come light-years from his first day in my family as a black ball huddled in a cage, he was still justifiably fearful of strange settings and sounds. He would let my mother carry him, but only if he could "escape" back to me at any instant. When he got overly excited, he would begin leaping and screaming and thrashing his arms around. In this frame of mind, he had no compunction against biting, and my mother's arms already bore the bruises of his teeth marks.

Before we got in the car on the way to the studio, with Kulu dressed in a striped blue shirt and a diaper, I called my bosses and begged reprieve one final time. It was not granted. "It's time for him to begin paying his way," they said. Paying his way??? Is he a slave who needs to pay his way? By the time we got to the studio and were made to wait until after the Gumby segment, Kulu was squirming in my arms, fussing and crawling all over me.

Do you remember *Romper Room?* It was a show where little kids did a sort of preschool thing on live television with Miss Nancy, or Miss Vicki, or whoever the star of the show was that year. This year, the host was Miss Maryanne, and this is how that particular segment went:

"Well, boys and girls, next we are in for a real treat! We

are going to welcome Miss Sue from the Zoo. She has a very, very special guest with her today." Boys and girls in dapper, pressed pants and fluffy little dresses "ooh and ahhh" as Kulu and I walk on stage and take a seat next to Miss Maryanne, who is sitting at a teacher's desk.

"Well hello, Miss Maryanne! Today I brought my new friend Kulu for a visit. He is a baby chimpanzee." Kulu stares and points at the overhead lights and fidgets anxiously in my arms. Trying to hold on to him is like trying to keep hold of a wet bar of soap. I offer him a bottle of apple juice and manage to get his attention for a moment, and there is the sound of a baby sucking. Then, Miss Maryanne does something we will all live to regret. She opens her desk drawer and brings out a hand mirror.

"Look, children, I have a mirror here! Why don't we see what Kulu thinks of it! Do you think Kulu has ever seen himself in a mirror?" She holds the mirror up in front of Kulu's face and catches us both completely off guard. But — hallejula! — it looks like Kulu is taking it all in stride.

"Look at that! Kulu is kissing himself in the mirror! Do you think he recognizes himself? Is he telling us he thinks he is a good boy?" Kulu gently kisses his image in the mirror. He seems quite happy and pleased with himself. Then, I see him notice Miss Maryanne's thumb, holding up the mirror to his face. I have a fraction of a second to think "Oh no..." before he leans forward, puts the thumb in his mouth, and bites down hard. There is a screech — not his — as blood spurts onto the mirror....

"Oh, boys and girls! Don't worry, Miss Maryanne's not hurt!" says Miss Maryanne while wrapping the end of her sweater around her thumb to stop the bleeding. "No, she's just surprised!" Kids begin shouting, a few start to cry. One scrambles under the table and hides. There is another screech; this time it is Kulu. He has wrestled away from me and is standing on the desk like King Kong, shouting at Miss Maryanne and waving his fists at the children. I grab him and without thinking, swat his bottom.

"No, Kulu! Stop that!" I have become a child abuser. More children start crying. The rest pile under their tables and put their arms over their heads like we're having an air raid drill.

"Now, boys and girls, see?! Sometimes when we are bad we need a spanking, and Miss Sue is spanking Kulu because he's being a bad boy right now." Bad boy my ass. He's been patient as Job and then some. And for that I am spanking him. I see this scene as if I have become astrally projected from my body: I am clutching Kulu, shamed to the bottom of my soul. Kulu is shouting at Miss Maryanne, who is trying to make sense of total bedlam.

"OOOH! Ooooh HOOOH!" Kulu leaps up and down, all the hair on his small body standing on end. He looks like a hissing cat, defending his small patch of turf on my lap, shaking curses at the Evil Mirror Woman.

The camera cuts to Gumby again. My father told me about this later. He was watching the whole thing on TV at the restaurant where he worked. So were all his co-workers. They cheered.

The *Romper Room* fiasco did nothing to deter my bosses' plans to make Kulu "earn his keep." A ferocious dance began, with me hop-skipping to buy Kulu time for rest and some resemblance of family life while my bosses jigged a fast tune of forced zoo enculturation, public appearances, and solitary time in a viewing cage. I was nineteen, as I said, and politically naive. My way of protecting Kulu was to get tense and belligerent with my bosses — a stupid ploy that served no one. I did whatever I could to finagle time together with Kulu, from spending my lunch times squinched up with him in his viewing cage to insisting that he continue to spend after hours at my home.

I got my way a little bit of the time, most likely because Kulu was happy with me. This made him so much more appealing to the public. It is hard to expect the public to pay for the privilege of watching a screeching, flailing, angry animal. The public wanted to see a happy baby, a cute hairy boy, and Kulu and I could conspire to deliver this charade, within certain limits.

I could see and feel the fine line between resignation and utter despair that Kulu walked each day. The stress he was subjected to showed in worry lines above his hairy brow and hunched his fragile shoulders. When a day had simply been too long, he would go back inside himself for comfort, masking his eyes with a vacant glaze, picking at his fingers, and "ooohing" to himself. Then I would pick up the pace of my own dodging dance, trying in the nighttime hours at home to give him back the spirit that was sucked from him at the zoo each day.

We had wonderful moments at home! Within the safety and security of those walls, Kulu allowed his rebel spirit to soar in a way he never could at the zoo. He loved to keep one eye on our cat so that he could nonchalantly grab at her tail when she walked within range. One night, I brought a box of lion cubs home for night feedings and spent the evening taking them away from Kulu, who would sneak off with them, one by one, hauling them out of the room by their scrawny tails.

I was braver in those days, and stupider. Although chimps do not like water, I thought it would be marvelous if I could get Kulu to enjoy baths. The zoo smell was overpowering— a rank and sweet odor of fermenting fruit and old monkey biscuits — and his black hair had gotten dull and sticky. One night after he had watched me taking tub baths for a few weeks and tasted lots of soapy bath water with his fingers, I impulsively lifted him into the tub and set him down on my stomach. The warm water touched his white-tufted bare bottom, and he burst out with a concerned hoot.

I forged ahead with confidence, pouring water from a plastic cup down his back while telling him in effervescent tones how wonderful baths can be. Kulu was willing to trust me to great lengths, so it was not until he was fully lathered up that he decided he'd had about enough and reached for the side wall of the tub. I turned and reached for his arm to pull him back, and he grabbed hold of the nearest thing that offered a steady grip, which was my right nipple. This made me instantly...nervous. Which in turn made him nervous, and he grabbed harder. As his nails sank into my flesh, I clenched my teeth and somehow managed to continue the bubbly baby talk while racing to rinse him clean. Of course, the rinsing and splashing only heaped more stress onto an already tense situation, so to calm himself, Kulu grabbed my other breast with his other hand and hung on still tighter.

I bolted from the tub and Kulu bolted from my arms, waggling his head side to side and shaking water everywhere. I applied Band-Aids to the right places and towel-dried Kulu, glad that no one but he — and he was mercifully without judgment — had witnessed my awesome lapse in common sense. He thought toweling was a good game. If you have never heard a chimp giggle, I can tell you that it is a joyous sound with all the mirth of a human laugh— like an excited, fast-whispered "Ha ha ha ha!" Yes, we lived to bathe together again, but I never again did it naked.

I occasionally took Kulu out on errands with me. I know animals are not allowed in stores, and I know that Kulu was an animal, but he was also my son, you see. So I would cover him head to toe with baby blankets, and no one was ever the wiser. Except for once. A very old woman came up beside me in the produce aisle one late afternoon and asked if she could see my baby. In a conspiratorial mood I complied. She looked down with her eyes wide and shining as the blanket fell away from Kulu's face. "Ohhh!" she said, "Is he your son? He is so beautiful!" I do not know if time and age had gently scooped her up and removed her from the cramped confines of this world, or if she was an angel. I smiled into her beaming face and said, "Yes, this is my son, Kulu. He is beautiful, isn't he?"

Soon afterward, I was fired from my zoo job. There were many reasons, and I'm sure my attitude was one of them. Without notice, I was asked to turn Kulu over to the zoo manager, who would take over his care. I don't want to go into this deeply. It is much too painful to revisit, and so I will keep this part of the writing as brief as I can. This is what happened in the course of the next three days: I handed Kulu over with all his clothes and toys and was told that I could still come to visit him when I wanted. Kulu's home care ended, and he was caged at night at the zoo across the room from two older chimps — four-year-olds who spent their days on Chimp Island. The young woman hired to replace me forgot to lock the cages of the two older chimps on Kulu's second night at the zoo. She found Kulu the next morning, huddled in the corner of the building with his ears bitten off, holding his entrails in his hands.

The two bigger chimps, curious and perhaps jealous of all the attention Kulu received, had left their unlocked cages that night and pulled Kulu from his. They bit and punched him. And with strong, inquisitive fingers, they had reached up into his rectum and pulled his insides out. Then they left him bleeding in the corner, crept back to their own cages, and closed the barred steel doors behind them.

The zoo manager called to tell me what had happened and to let me know that Kulu was still alive. The zoo vet had performed a miracle of surgery on him, and everyone was keeping their fingers crossed that a fatal infection would not set in. I was told that it took one hundred fifty stitches to sew him up again, and that part of his bowel had been removed. The manager told me that it would be too traumatic for Kulu if I visited him in his fragile state and asked me to keep away so that he could adjust to his new handlers and heal. But I visited him secretly three days later. From a distance, I saw him sitting in the ticket office on the manager's lap. He was looking carefully at a yellow plastic ball in his hands, turning it over and over. Scabs had replaced his ears, and he was covered from the waist down in white bandages. Swallowing hard, I went away and stayed away.

A year passed, most of which I spent out of state. I kept in intermittent contact with the zoo, so I knew Kulu had survived, had been moved eventually to Chimp Island as the older chimps were sold off, and that he had a new "girl-friend" — a female chimp his own age for company. And so one summer day when the afternoon shadows were long and my heart was strong enough to be rebroken, I went to the zoo, bought my ticket, and found myself standing at the railing in front of Chimp Island. I recognized Kulu instantly, not because of the crimped ears but because he had been my son and I knew his posture and his presence. I stood looking at him for a long time across the moat before he ever saw me. When he eventually looked my way, it was with eyes that indicated no recognition. He turned his back to me and sat chewing a monkey biscuit. I stood there watching his shoulders move, flooded with feelings for which I have no words at all. "Loss," "relief," "grief" — none are close.

After a time, he turned to face me. Putting aside the monkey biscuit, he walked on two legs closer to the edge of Chimp Island and sat on his haunches, looking into my face. He turned away again, only to face me once more with a look of confusion, dismissal. The other visitors had moved on and there was no one at the railing but me. Tears were pouring down my face, and for a moment, I couldn't see anything. I didn't realize he had gotten to his feet and walked to the supporting beam that was directly across the moat from me. When I wiped my face on my sleeve, it was just in time to see him take hold of the steel beam with one arm, and reach … reach across the moat to me with his other hand, fingers stretched out to span the distance between us. My arm reached out reflexively in return, and I stood up on my toes to reach as far across the shallow water as I could stretch myself. I called out his name in a whisper, and he called back to me, his lips forming a soft "O." His eyes were soft and large and he thrust his small face toward me. I was weeping hard, gulping down tears and mucous.

The hand that touched the back of my shoulder gave me a start, and I leaped back from the guardrail. It was the new manager, a man I had met several times before I had lost my job at the zoo. He was holding a pair of waders, bulky brown things we always used to wade over to the island. "I remember you. Why don't you go visit him for a while," he said, nodding toward Kulu. Surprised and grateful, I took the waders and he turned away smiling. "Take your time," he called back to me.

I was halfway across the water when Kulu leaped up into my arms, wrapping his hands around my torso, "Ooohhing" over and over. I carried him over near the post and leaned against it, cradling him in my arms, crying. The warmth of his small, clutching hands was familiar, the sticky sweet smell of him as known to me as my own body scent. I put my head against his and we spoke to each other in murmurs and sighs. He put his fingers on my face, poked one up my nose, pulled gently at my lower lip, and extended his soft rubbery chimp lips up to mine in a kiss.

The shadows lengthened and embraced us. It was a long time before I put him down again. I did not release him until he indicated that he wanted to go, and then I let him loose

only hesitantly. He walked off on all fours over to his companion and, with his eyes still on me, began gently preening the
hairs of her arm, as he had once done for me. The look on his
face was peaceful and soft, and when I turned to slosh my way
back across the moat, he hooted to me. It was his mother call,
and I heard it vibrate like a violin string inside me.

Kept Relations

OWNERSHIP, COMPANIONSHIP, AND BONDAGE

*"In such places," (he went on at last) "where animals are simply
penned up, they are almost always more thoughtful than their
cousins in the wild. This is because even the dimmest of them
cannot help but sense that something is very wrong with this style
of living. . . . Why? 'Why, why, why, why, why, why?' the tiger
asks itself hour after hour, day after day, year after year,
as it treads its endless path behind the bars of its cage."*

— Daniel Quinn, *Ishmael*

I dressed as a vulture: mask, cloak, and attitude. Fourteen of
us were coming to the climax of our two-day workshop
called "The Council of All Beings." It was time for the
Council part of the weekend, where we would each represent
and speak for some aspect of nature that had chosen to speak
through us. Our time together as a group had been reflective
and profound, full of humor, songs, and sorrows. Going
alone out into the California oak hills where the Council was
hosted, each of us found our "voice." Mine was the voice of
Buzzard, renewer of all things, recycler of death and loss into
life and energy, witness to bones, cleanser of the Earth.

The mask I'd made with cardboard and cloth was awesome, and when I put it on, I felt myself instinctively hunch
like a vulture. It was three in the afternoon when we

gathered to sit in the dirt around a stack of stones and speak until we were all done. I remember so many beings represented around the circle that day — from seeds to soil to mountains, ants to woodpeckers — but the one I remember most vividly was the being who sat with a paper bag over her head, two eye holes punched in the center, and black lines running from top to bottom of the wrinkled sack. When she finally spoke, I understood that the black lines were the bars of a prison. "I speak today," she said quietly, "for all animals in bondage."

Bondage? This is a bit dramatic, I thought. But long after the Council was over and I was back to my daily life, I remembered that wrinkled bag and the black bars. The image would not leave me alone: animals in bondage. Bondage. My dictionary defines the word as "involuntary personal service." I thought about animals kept in laboratories, in circuses, in zoos, in rodeos, in breeding cages, and I felt the sadness and helplessness of it all. But when I looked into the eyes of my precious dogs and saw the bars running down over their eyes from top to bottom, I knew that woman had changed my life and my thinking forever.

There is a dialogue among some people who keep animals, a dialogue of astonishment and disbelief at the radical notion of some animal activist groups that animals should not be kept as "pets" — not at all, ever. I listen to the outrage of the animal owners and the defiance of the radicals, and I understand the polar positions of both. That is, I *feel* them both. I have kept animals all my life, and I have worked for organizations that keep them, such as zoos, shelters, kennels, horse farms, and pet shops. My life has been

defined by the animals I have known and kept. I have rescued many animals from conditions of misery and sickness,
and those animals have gone on to other homes where they
were kept and loved by others. If you look over my writing,
you will see that I try to avoid the word "ownership" in
regard to the animals I keep. I hate that word. It shames me.
And so I say animals are my family, my companions, my
teachers. But the truth is, for the most part, I own them. I
am their keeper, their master — a more benevolent master
than some, but a master nonetheless.

In his famous speech, Chief Seattle questions the white
culture's notion of owning the Earth, the ground — a concept unknown to his people. We have some funny words for
the Earth that I suspect have no equivalents in most indigenous cultures: We call the Earth "property" or "real estate."
But the idea of ownership is a sticky thing. The wider we
humans throw our net of ownership, the smaller our potential for wholeness becomes. Our world of relationships is one
of many interior and exterior worlds that shrink before the
notion of ownership. A master is limited to certain kinds of
relationships with his servants. If master and servant move
beyond this limit, cultural uproar and scandal ensue. In this
way, we keep ourselves emotionally secure and stunted in our
little, cramped relational boxes.

The keeping of animals is a concept with many, many
faces. One is the face of the kept one, the other of the keeper.
Still another is the face of the particular society that defines
the rules and standards and integrity of the keeping. If I do
not look into all these faces, if I shy away, I can stay easy and
safe in my skin. But my relationship with Strongheart, my

dog, will be far less than whole, and our opportunities for communion and joy chopped far short of what is possible. Limitations on any kind of thinking diminish our potential for wholeness. Sometimes these limitations are needed to protect a fragile or wounded psyche, but most often, the conservative nature of our inner inquiry is more a matter of comfort and habit.

Looking at the various faces of ownership allows a deeper reflection, wherein lurks a paradox: Admitting my ownership over my dog is not something I like to think about. Thinking about the restrictions and mastery that my ownership exerts over Strongheart humiliates and frustrates me. Yet if I don't consider the owner-bondage question, I am short-changing us both.

To find greater freedom and honesty in our relationship, I have to step onto ground that hurts my heart and soul. I have to concede that my beloved Strongheart has no autonomy over his own life in any way. When he eats, where he poops, where and when he sleeps, plays, visits, or buries a bone are all determined by me. If I don't like the weather, he doesn't get to go for his walk. And when that walk happens is never his say, anyhow. He is fed, housed, loved, and protected, and his life is not his own. His small choices are made within the tight parameters of my choices, my needs, my whims, my fantasies about what he needs or wants. I know that his own choices for himself would be far different. He would choose to run free and to sniff new ground for hours. He would choose to mate, had I not taken his testicles away, and to fight, and to hunt rabbits and voles and eat them down raw and hot. He would choose to tell me "no" in many ways. He would visit me when he wanted, and he would not come home each night.

In his heart and being, Strongheart is a creature who is perfectly capable of finding food for himself and deciding how and where to spend his days. Every living thing that has been created by the One is gifted with at least these skills for life and choice. But Strongheart will never have that chance to be his bigger, freer self. His life is given over to involuntary personal servitude. It is this way with any animal we keep.

At a horse training retreat, I listened across the dinner table as a woman chattered about her show horse: "He lives the life of luxury — an air-conditioned barn, grain every day, baths, brushing. I think the least he owes me a good ride now and then."

Before I could stop the words, they fell bluntly out of my mouth, "He owes you nothing." I looked down at the peas on my plate and felt my cheeks go red. Conversation was dropped with a thud. When it started up again, we all talked animatedly about the meaning of ownership and who owes us what. The table was split. There were those of us who felt that in exchange for food, shelter, and love, it was right to ask certain things of the animals in our care, referring particularly to horses. Others of us sat with the vision of Horse Spirit, a being of wind and distance and speed, forced to stand for days at a time in a stall — albeit a clean stall with good water and regular food and with occasional turnouts for exercise. We reached no consensus that night.

I think about Kulu. It's been more than thirty years since I last saw him at our meeting at the moat, and I ask myself:

Is he still alive? Who might he have been if he had experienced even one day of free choice in his life? What is it like to be watched constantly by strangers, every day? Would any creature choose bondage? How can I live with this?

Given a choice, I believe that few, if any, animals would elect to live in zoos, laboratories, stalls, or cages. And, honestly, I don't think many of them would even choose to live in our homes. The comfort of human companionship is meaningful to domestic animals because we have twisted their wild nature and made our company of value to them. In their own wild souls and in harmony with their original instructions, they have no need to live with us. The need is ours for them. And I find this idea mortifying, humbling, and weighted mightily in a huge responsibility that is sometimes too heavy for me to shoulder.

Do I believe we should no longer own animals? That all animals are in some sort of bondage to us? Yes, yes, down to my very bones I believe this. Fighting for laws to ensure the humane care of animals, while vital and necessary, is to me sadly akin to repairing shattered bridges over rivers the Holy One never granted us license to cross. If I were Queen of the World and could snap my fingers and make it so, I would snap away and release all animals peacefully. None of them would suffer from the freedom. Instead, they would go back into the world that is their true Mother, and they would be loved in life and death by her alone. As Queen, I would declare it law that our interactions with all of our relations be founded upon compassion, mystery, and respect, rather than by involuntary service. Some creatures would elect to stay with us, and some wouldn't.

I would release the animals not only for their good, but for the resurrection of our own wild souls. It is not natural to be a keeper, a jailer, a lord, a master. It was never written this way in any creature's original instructions. I would liberate us humans, as well, from our paradoxical four-sided boxes of ownership-bondage-stewardship-need into a landscape of greater breathing and broader loving and grander healing. We would walk then, instead of ride, and we would carry our own burdens on the path. We would fight our own battles instead of sending horses and dogs and dolphins to kill for us and beside us. And we would be the better for it.

Without equivocation, I believe in the relinquishment of the terrible burden of ownership of animals, just as much as I believe I will never see such a world in my lifetime. We may not yet be able to create a world without bondage, but we can lay down this toxic worldview, now, both individually and collectively. The freedom of all animals is not a *condition* in which we live, but it is a *mind-set* we can hold, now. And that is the root of change.

There are dogs and cats who need homes now, today, and some of them will come to live in mine and some in yours. It is better to care for them than to let them fend for themselves on the streets. I cannot — will not — let Strongheart run free. I cannot release all the animals in laboratories, or make the Chinese stop torturing and imprisoning bears for their bile. I cannot free all the factory-farmed chickens of the world. But there is one huge thing I can do, and I can do it right now. I can release my belief in the idea that it is right and proper for humans to *own* animals. And I do this as many times a day as the concept comes to me, which is often. I release the idea whenever I place my dogs' food bowls on the floor, whenever I slip on Strongheart's muzzle, whenever I choose not to visit the rodeo or the zoo, whenever I see a cow standing alone on a manure heap. Releasing this idea allows me to live with the awareness of and responsibility for the restriction of all my relations with much deeper humility.

Sometimes the most powerful thing we can do is to think, long and hard. Changing our ideas about the world is not an outer activity, but the inner activity from which all outer action stems. Quantum physics is telling us that consciousness — the mind — is the birthplace of action. Our arm does not lift until we think it so. Our world does not change until we imagine it so. So right now, my main way of enacting the tenet of nonownership of other lives is, frankly, to think about it and talk about it. In doing just this much — this huge much — my relationship with animals and nature is transformed into one of greater respect, depth, and equality of soul. And the rest of my life changes in ways that are both tiny and immense.

I honor all those who keep animals in kindness and humility. I say prayers both for the activists who wish no animal had to live at the command of a human and for the dedicated animal keepers who love their animals deeply and mindfully. I remind myself often that Strongheart's days and nights are not his own, and that his gifts of acceptance, love, and willingness come to me because he is a far more gracious and gentle captive than I would ever be.

Somewhere in a zoo in this country, Kulu might still be alive. He would be an old silverback by now, with stumpy, serrated ears. If you should ever see him, please tell him that while I was his keeper, I was also his adoring mother. Tell him that I am sorry for the ghostly bars that separate us and hurt us both. Tell him that I bear witness for him and for all my relations. It is the largest thing I can do, this feeling, remembering, and this reflection. Tell him he is still my relative.

A Practice

Think. Feel. Share your stories. Aho, Mitaku Oyasin.

Notes

Introduction

1.   Michael Cohen, *Well Mind, Well Earth* (Roche Harbor, Wash.: World Peace University Press, 1997), 11.

Chapter 1: Misty

Epigraph, page 12: Barry Lopez, *Crow and Weasel* (San Francisco: North Point Press, 1990).

Chapter 3: The Goddess and the Chicken

Epigraph, page 53: Hilary Hart, *The Unknown She: Eight Faces of an Emerging Consciousness* (Chicago: Independent Publishers Group, 2003).

1.   Marion Woodman, *Leaving My Father's House: A Journey to Conscious Femininity* (Boston: Shambhala Publications, 1992), 3.

Chapter 5: Strongheart

Epigraph, page 93: Jean Shinoda Bolen, *Crossing to Avalon: A Woman's Midlife Pilgrimage* (San Francisco: HarperSan Francisco, reprint, 1995), 17.

1. Michael Cohen, *Reconnecting with Nature: Finding Wellness through Restoring Your Bond with the Earth* (Corvalis, Ore.: Ecopress, 1997), 85.

Chapter 6: Number 10

Epigraph, pages 110–111: Ursula K. Le Guin, "She Unnames Them," from *Buffalo Gals and Other Animal Presences* (New York: New American Library, reprint, 1990).

Chapter 7: River Elk

Epigraph, page 127: Denise Linn, *The Secret Language of Signs: How to Interpret the Coincidences and Symbols in Your Life* (New York: Ballantine, 1996), 3.

Chapter 8: Tarantulove

Epigraph, page 144: Jelalludin Rumi, "The Gift," in *News of the Universe: Poems of Twofold Consciousness,* ed. Robert Bly (San Francisco: Sierra Club Books, reprint, 1995).
1. Joanne Elizabeth Lauck, *The Voice of the Infinite in the Small: Re-Visioning the Insect-Human Connection* (Boston: Shambhala Publications, rev. ed., 2002), 13–14.
2. Robert A. Johnson, *We: Understanding the Psychology of Romantic Love* (San Francisco: HarperCollins, 1983).

Chapter 9: Fashion

1. Maureen Murdock, *The Heroine's Journey: Reclaiming the Wise Woman Within* (Boston: Shambhala Publications, 1990), 17.

Chapter 10: Kulu

Epigraph, page 198: Daniel Quinn, *Ishmael: An Adventure of the Mind and Spirit* (New York: Bantam, 1995).

Resources

These are the organizations and books that have helped me grow along this particular part of the journey. I am keeping this list short, in the hope that its brevity will encourage you to explore and taste everything on it. While very different in their offerings, all these resources have come together for me in a seamless and comforting alchemical blend of hope and healing. Together, they have transformed me — near painlessly — from the inside out. I can think of no greater recommendation than that.

Organizations

PROJECT NATURE CONNECT

Dr. Michael Cohen, the founder of Project Nature Connect and the Natural Systems Thinking Process, is a maverick genius whose work in restoring our sensory connection with nature, for our benefit and hers, changed my worldview in six weeks, bringing me profound new tools for healing, for living, and for working sanely in an insane world. He facilitates an online degree and study program in applied ecopsychology that is utterly unique and astonishingly applicable to everyday life. I cannot recommend his programs and books highly enough. I don't believe there is any part of my work to come that will not be affected by his work and teachings. I encourage you — no, I beseech you — to sign up for his online orientation course. Tell him I sent you.

Dr. Michael Cohen
Institute of Global Education
Box 1605
Friday Harbor, WA 98250
360.378.6313

THE RIVERWIND FOUNDATION

This small nonprofit foundation and close community of teachers, writers, and facilitators is the vehicle through which my work is held and shared in the world. Over a five-year period, RiverWind has become my organizational home for exploring a new — or perhaps very ancient — way of being in the world: a place for expanding our human capacity for relationships, for interdependence, and for community in its most healthy sense. The hallmark of RiverWind is our Annual Kindred Spirit retreat, where we put to work everything we continue to learn each year about bringing community and a sense of sacredness to each and every aspect of life. If you have felt like an alien on Earth, you may find your family here.

The RiverWind Foundation
Box 13190
Jackson, WY 83002
800.942.4004

Books

The Power of Now, by Eckhart Tolle (Takes you up)
Soulcraft, by Bill Plotkin (Takes you in)
The Call, by Oriah Mountain Dreamer (Blends the two)

About the Author

Susan Chernak McElroy's classic work, *Animals as Teachers and Healers,* remains an international hallmark in the literature of human-animal relationships. With its captivating blend of story, unflinching vulnerability, and provocative reflection, her writing continues to break new ground in exploring our inherently sacred connections with nature, animals, Earth, and the human soul. For more information on her books, lectures, and work, please visit her Website at susanchernakmcelroy.com.

New World Library is dedicated to
publishing books and audio products
that inspire and challenge us to improve
the quality of our lives and our world.

Our products are available
in bookstores everywhere.
For our catalog, please contact:

New World Library
14 Pamaron Way
Novato, California 94949

Phone: (415) 884-2100 or (800) 972-6657
Catalog requests: Ext. 50
Orders: Ext. 52
Fax: (415) 884-2199

E-mail: escort@newworldlibrary.com
Website: www.newworldlibrary.com